COCKTAIL PARTIES, STRAIGHT UP!

easy hors D'oeuvres, Delicious Drinks, and inspired ideas for entertaining with style

Lauren Purcell and Anne Purcell Grissinger

WILEY

John Wiley & Sons, Inc.

Published by John Wiley & Sons, Inc., Hoboken, New Jersey

Published simultaneously in Canada

For general information about our other products and services, please contact our Customer Care Department within the United States at (800) 762-2974, outside the United States at (317) 572-3993 or fax (317) 572-4002.

Wiley also publishes its books in a variety of electronic formats. Some content that appears in print may not be available in electronic books. For more information about Wiley products, visit our web site at www.wiley.com.

Library of Congress Cataloging-in-Publication Data:
Purcell, Lauren.
  Cocktail parties, straight up! : easy hors d'oeuvres, delicious drinks, and inspired ideas for entertaining with style / Lauren Purcell and Anne Purcell Grissinger.
      p. cm.
    Includes index.
    ISBN 0-764-55896-X (pbk.)
  1. Cocktail parties. 2. Entertaining. I. Grissinger, Anne Purcell. II. Title.
    TX731.P863 2005
    642'.4—dc22   2005001266

Illustrations by Sujean Rim

Printed in the United States of America

10 9 8 7 6 5 4 3 2 1

CONTENTS

THE PARTIES

FOR OUR MOTHER,
the original dispenser of straight-up advice

ACKNOWLEDGMENTS

A crowd of people helped make this book happen. We'd like to raise a glass to:

Cheryl Kramer, Marge Perry, and Nina Willdorf, whose expertise and insightful advice made every page far better.

Our invaluable team of recipe testers, who tried out our hors d'oeuvres in their own kitchens and at their own parties: Stephanie Albertson, Sara Austin, Ellen Benson, Laura Bowman, Meg D'Incecco, Bobbie Kittleson, Kathryn Kranhold, Richard McKilligan, Jennifer Riffle, Wendy Cooper Roche, Janet Shearer, Corrie Thomas, Patti Wolter, and especially our mom, Michele Purcell, who cooked up a storm on our behalf and was always on the other end of the phone when we had a crisis in the kitchen.

Diana Biederman, Hilary Black, and Sadie Van Gelder, who offered early encouragement; Philip Kiracofe, whose martini party inspired the one in this book; and the family, friends, and colleagues who shared their advice, contacts, recipes, and support: the Bartow-Lakeland cocktail party crowd, Francesca Castagnoli, Wendy Marcus, David Bonom, Wendy Bounds, Diane VanDusen, Tim Bogardus, Jeanne and Rich Grissinger, and Carolynn Carreño.

R.J. Grissinger, for enduring long weekends alone and dinners made up entirely of hors d'oeuvres.

Our editor, Linda Ingroia, and our agent, Andrew Stuart, for believing in this project from the start; Rachel Bartlett and everyone at Wiley who had a hand in making it a reality; and our talented illustrator, Sujean Rim.

And finally, every guest who's ever attended a Purcell Sisters party. This book would not exist without you.

Cheers!

Lauren and Anne

INTRODUCTION
WHO WE ARE AND WHY WE WROTE THIS BOOK

The first cocktail party we ever threw—in the apartment we shared when we moved to New York City—was not a success. Oh, nothing particularly dreadful happened. The food tasted fine, the drinks flowed freely. But the party just never seemed to jell. Lauren's friends (journalists, mostly) talked shop on one side of the living room, while Anne's friends (financial types, mostly) congregated on the other side. We'd had visions of everyone mingling animatedly. Maybe dancing would spontaneously break out! Perhaps someone would meet his true love at our party and we'd be toasted at their wedding! But no. Our guests just placidly munched their hors d'oeuvres and traded chit-chat with people they already knew. We were crushed.

But we were also determined. We grew up in the small-town South, land of lawn parties and mint juleps; it would be very nearly traitorous not to be good hosts. Plus, we remembered the parties our parents threw when we were kids, and how magical they seemed. We would sneak out into the hallway long after we'd been sent to bed and peek at the grown-ups all dressed up, smiling and laughing, obviously having a wonderful time. When we became grown-ups ourselves, we wanted to recreate that atmosphere.

We envisioned a warm and friendly event where style and sociability would come together. Delicious food and drinks were essential, of course, but we also wanted our parties to have that indefinable element of connectedness, when everyone is swept up in the mood of the evening, and the guests seem to meet effortlessly and forget that they'd planned to stay only an hour.

We were long on ideas, but after our disappointing debut, a little short on confidence. So we went looking for instruction. At a bookstore near our apartment, we spent an entire Saturday searching through shelf after shelf of how-to-entertain books—yet we came away disappointed. The books we found had either dauntingly elaborate instructions that didn't seem doable for two girls with day jobs, or advice so frustratingly vague that we wondered if crucial pages had been ripped out. On how many people to invite, for instance, one book advised that the "room should not feel empty, and at the same time not feel over-crowded." *But what does that mean, exactly?!* What we were after was something more concrete—a recommended number of guests. But it was nowhere to be found. Then there were the books that assumed that we had lots of time and money to waste: "Paint the room red for a dose of instant sultriness." *You call that instant?!* Worse still were the books that drew us in by promising to make party-throwing quick and easy. Unfortunately, the advice they contained didn't reduce our stress; it just made us roll our eyes. No time to cook? No problem, one book assured us. Just spruce up takeout food by sprinkling it with the petals of edible flowers. *Oh sure,* those *are a cinch to find!*

We craved a book—even just a chapter or two—whose advice would feel down-to-earth and doable for people like us. We're capable cooks, not trained chefs or caterers. We're enthusiastic cocktail drinkers, but by no means professional "mixologists." We have full-time jobs, not full-time staffs. And we host our parties not in a mansion but in a Manhattan apartment with room for two people in the kitchen *if* they suck in their stomachs.

Clearly, we were on our own. So we experimented: Over the next 10 years, we tried out hundreds of hors d'oeuvre recipes, discarding many of them and fine-tuning the rest. We tinkered with the recipes for classic cocktails and invented our own. We endlessly brainstormed creative ways to get guests mingling. And we road-tested everything, throwing parties of all sorts and sizes and making loads of notes about what worked and what didn't. Our own parties weren't the only ones we dissected. Every invitation we received was an opportunity to pick up hostessing hints or hors d'oeuvre ideas. At a friend's annual Christmas party, we noted that she put the bar and the buffet table in separate rooms—a great way to get guests to spread out over the entire house instead of crowding into one area. At a wedding reception, we fell in love with *gougères*, a classic French cheese hors d'oeuvre, and we ended up developing a version of it ourselves (Savory Cheese Puffs, page 84).

The result of all our efforts? You're holding it in your hands. *Cocktail Parties, Straight Up! Easy Hors D'oeuvres, Delicious Drinks, and Inspired Ideas for Entertaining with Style* captures our experiences and provides straightforward answers to the questions we ourselves asked in our early party-throwing years. This is the no-nonsense advice you would give your sister or best friend if she asked you for hostessing how-tos. You'd share all your secrets and shortcuts, dig out your fool-proof recipes. You'd give her detailed practical advice, not vague suggestions. You would help her head off mishaps that you had suffered through already. (Remember that party when you ran out of ice after only an hour? Or the time you underestimated how much glassware you needed and your guests had to drink cocktails out of coffee mugs?) *Cocktail Parties, Straight Up!* is like having a trusted, tell-it-like-it-is sister by your side. Or, as it happens, two sisters.

THIS BOOK IS FOR YOU IF...

...you're new to throwing cocktail parties and you want step-by-step instructions.

Each of the 12 party chapters in this book contains the complete blueprint for a cocktail party. No need to rifle through cookbooks trying to figure out what to serve: We've carefully crafted the menu for each party, putting together exactly the right mix of hors d'oeuvres *and* thinking about the prep time for each recipe so that you don't end up panicked and perspiring in the kitchen.

Each chapter also includes the recipe for one or more signature cocktails—the simplest way we know to make a party feel special and at the same time streamline bartending duties. Plus, in every party, we've solved the beginning host's "will people have fun?" worries by giving you step-by-step instructions for a Conversation Kick-Starter, our fun, foolproof way to get guests to meet, mingle, and make friends.

We've mapped it all out, from start to finish. All you have to do is choose which party to start with.

. . . you're not new to party-throwing, but you want to raise your hostess confidence level.

Maybe you've already got some hors d'oeuvres recipes you know are big hits. Or you feel pretty secure in your ability to get guests into the groove of a party. Then you can use this book "à la carte," mixing and matching the elements that most appeal to you from various parties. Plus, throughout the book, we share with you our Sisters' Secrets to Confident Hostessing, which will help you navigate the finer points of throwing a successful cocktail party, from before the first guest arrives (see our discussion of "the 6:30 friend" on page 46) till the last one leaves (on page 150, we tell you how to end a party gracefully). By filling in the gaps in your knowledge, we will turn you from competent hostess to entertaining expert.

. . . you're a veteran hostess who could use an idea infusion.

Maybe you've thrown tons of parties, but you're feeling the need for a few new twists to shake you out of your entertaining rut. That's exactly why we created our unique brand of "gently themed" parties—each with a mingle-encouraging Conversation Kick-Starter: so your guests will be transported out of their workaday worlds and swept up in the novelty of the evening.

Whoever you are, let this book inspire you!

HOW TO GET ORGANIZED
EVERY PARTY'S
3 ESSENTIAL ELEMENTS

When we began writing this book, we did a little informal poll of our friends: Why, we wanted to know, did so few of them ever throw a cocktail party themselves? The answer, overwhelmingly, was: *It's just too overwhelming!* They all enjoyed going to cocktail parties, but hosting one? That sounded hard. As more than one person said: *I wouldn't even know where to begin.* Well, here's where to begin, and it's not nearly as hard as you may have thought. We've distilled the cocktail party into its three essential elements—food, drinks, and guests—and developed realistic strategies for getting a handle on each one. Our guidelines will guarantee that *any* party you throw will be a big success.

Essential element #1
the food

In every one of the 12 parties in this book, we've provided a carefully thought-out menu with easy-to-follow recipes. Every menu adheres to our Rule of Five, which results in a perfect mix of hors d'oeuvres and ensures that you, the host, will be able to prepare all the food yourself—much of it a few days before the party—without feeling overwhelmed. We've shared that rule with you below, so you can devise your own menus, and we've also provided the Hors D'oeuvres Estimator, our ultra-reliable rule of thumb for how much food to make.

HOW TO CREATE THE PERFECT MENU: THE RULE OF FIVE

Who in the world came up with the idea that the more guests you have, the more types of hors d'oeuvres you should offer? It just doesn't make sense: Each guest still has only one mouth. Sure, you need a larger amount of each item, but what's the point of a wider variety other than to increase the time you're stuck in the kitchen and send your stress level through the roof?

Instead, use our foolproof Rule of Five: For every party, no matter how large or small, we create a menu with five different hors d'oeuvres:

- *One "heavy,"* so that guests who skip dinner still feel satisfied.

- *One either "heavy" or "medium."* If you expect the party to go long or your guests to be big eaters, lean toward a heavier second hors d'oeuvre.

- *One "medium."* This is often our vegetarian hors d'oeuvre or a dip.

- *One lighter choice,* such as crudités, for nibblers.

- *One bowl item,* such as nuts or olives, that can go in multiple bowls around the party so that guests can grab a little bite no matter where they are in the room.

This mix makes for a menu that's easily doable by one person, yet provides enough variety to look impressive and please every guest. Each party menu in this book is built around the Rule of Five, and we've also sorted all the recipes into a heavy/medium/light/bowl list (see page 8) so you can easily mix and match recipes from different parties to create menus of your own.

HOW MUCH FOOD YOU'LL NEED: THE HORS D'OEUVRES ESTIMATOR

When it comes to food, what's more important than a wide variety is a gracious plenty. In the olden days (whenever that was), cocktail parties occupied a defined time slot, often only two hours long, and it was expected that guests would go from the party on to dinner. When we host a party, we want our friends to come and stay for the whole evening. Our start time is usually 7 p.m., and we like to provide enough food so that guests feel satisfied even without a sit-down meal. We use the following formula, though obviously, you should adjust this based on whether your guest list includes a team of football players or, conversely, the local ballet troupe.

- *Heavy hors d'oeuvres*—4 to 5 pieces per guest

- *Heavy/medium hors d'oeuvres*—4 to 5 pieces per guest

- *Medium hors d'oeuvres (such as dip)*—4 to 5 pieces or ¼ cup of dip per guest

With dips, provide tons of bread, crackers, or other dip vehicles. They're cheap and easy to prepare—there should be no reason to run out of them.

- *Light hors d'oeuvres (such as crudités)*—5 to 6 pieces per guest

- *Bowl foods*—As a rule of thumb, we place 1 bowl for every 7 or 8 guests and keep them filled all night.

HOW IN THE WORLD WILL YOU GET IT ALL DONE? THE MAKE-AHEAD FACTOR

Maybe you've been there. We certainly have: The clock is ticking, you have 15 minutes until the first guest is due to arrive, and you're frantically trying to pull

THE RECIPES

Heavy Hors D'oeuvres

Asian Chicken Meatballs with Sweet-Sour Sauce, 109
Baby Lamb Chops with Rosemary Mustard Cream, 135
Beef Tenderloin and Pearl Onion Skewers, 36
Bite-Size Crab Cakes with Lemon Caper Mayo, 68
Chicken and Red Onion in Phyllo Cups, 69
Chicken Satay with Peanut Sauce, 147
Coconut Curry Scallops, 149
Cuban Sandwiches Pequeños, 165
Empanaditas, 120
Mexican Black Bean Quesadillas, 26
Moroccan Lamb Meatballs with Dill Sauce, 24
Peppery Shrimp, 108
Pork Tenderloin Sandwiches Two Ways, 92
Shrimp and Polenta Wedges, 138
Shrimp with Spicy Lime Dip, 157
Spicy Sausage Squares, 58
Steak Tartare, 48
Tandoori Lamb with Cumin Dipping Sauce, 80

Medium Hors D'oeuvres

Arepas with Pink Pickled Onions, 162
Asparagus Parmesan Bites, 49
Bacon Blue Cheese Dip, 60
Caramelized Onion Jam on Toast with Brie, 59
Caramelized Onion Tarts, 160
Chickpea Cilantro Dip, 152
Creamy Crab Dip with Jicama Spears, 126
Crostini with Tapenade, 83
Cucumber Goat Cheese Spread, 111
Goat Cheese and Leek Croustades, 122
Italian Baked Ravioli, 27
Olive Crostini with White Truffle Oil, 47
Seared Tuna and Cucumber Brochettes, 94
Smoked Trout Spread, 40
Sun-dried Tomato and Ricotta Torte Trio, 95
Sweet Potato Spread, 140
Tomato Sage Baby Brioches, 159
Top-Your-Own New Potatoes, 71
Wild Mushroom Tartlets, 38
Zesty Baked Zucchini Squares, 82

Light Hors D'oeuvres

Artichoke and Green Olive Dip, 125
Artichoke Hearts with Cucumber Aïoli, 51
Asparagus Spears with Lemon Dipping Sauce, 41
Crudités with Carrot-Ginger Dip, 112
Crudités with Indian Curry Dip, 28
Fennel-Spiced Cauliflower Florets, 97
Fresh Tomato Bruschetta, 73
Hearts of Palm, 158
Melon and Prosciutto Skewers, 61
Pineapple Salsa with Plantain Chips, 151
Savory Cheese Puffs, 84
Tomato-Basil-Mozzarella Skewers with Basil Oil, 141

Bowl Foods

Champagne-Marinated Grapes, 142
Fortune Cookies, 113
Greek Olives, 29
Green M&M's, 52
Lemon-Glazed Pecans, 42
Macadamia Nuts, 152
Pistachios, 127
Potato Chips, 166
Spiced Bar Nuts, 98
Supercharged Chex Mix, 62
Wasabi-Crusted Peas, 74
Wine Crackers, 85

together several complicated dishes. In *Cocktail Parties, Straight Up!* we've eliminated that problem. Each hors d'oeuvre recipe we've provided can be made at least partially and often entirely ahead of time, ensuring that you, the host, get to enjoy your own party, not just man the stove. We applied this crucial cocktail-party test to recipes we created on our own, inherited from family, or borrowed from friends, as well as those from restaurants, cookbooks, and magazines like *Gourmet* that we've been clipping and collecting for years. When a recipe was complicated, or required lots of last-minute attention, we adapted and streamlined it. Look for "The Make-Ahead Factor" in every recipe in the book. In addition, for many hors d'oeuvres, we've suggested shortcuts—look for "No Effort/Low Effort/Mo' Effort" — that will help make party prep even quicker.

ESSENTIAL ELEMENT #2
THE DRINKS

What would a cocktail party be without cocktails? (Answer: over by 8 p.m.) In each party, we give you the recipe for a delicious signature cocktail or, depending on the party, more than one. Designating a specific drink for each event makes the evening feel special, plus it provides a simple and ingenious conversation starter—a way to get guests in the party mood. (There's just something about everyone standing around drinking Pink Panthers—the signature cocktail in the Cartoons and Cocktails party—that breaks the ice the way vodka tonics never could.) Serving a signature cocktail also makes your job as hostess easier in two important ways: (1) Having a featured drink to offer guests eases the need to provide every other conceivable kind of liquor on your bar. Instead, you can use our Two-Bottle Bar rule and save yourself considerable effort and expense. (2) You can make the signature cocktail ahead of time by the pitcher (use our handy conversion chart, page 12), saving you from having to bartend during the party.

HOW TO STOCK YOUR BAR WITHOUT GOING BROKE: THE TWO-BOTTLE BAR

Stocking the bar sounds pretty simple until you stand in the liquor store and realize that even if you stick with "the basics" you're talking about gin, vodka, rum, tequila, Scotch, and bourbon—well over a hundred dollars' worth even if you don't buy premium brands. And if you're tempted to add in flavored vodkas or single-malt whiskeys or other non-basic booze options, your bill will quickly escalate.

To the rescue: our Two-Bottle Bar rule, which holds that when you serve a signature cocktail, there's no need to also provide an exhaustive selection of liquors. Instead, provide wine and beer (we'll give you some help with quantities below) and stock the bar with two kinds of liquor. That way, every guest will find something he or she likes to drink, and *you'll* find that you still have money in your checking account.

But which liquors? Well, of course it depends on what your friends like to drink. If there's a rage for rum at the moment, by all means, lay in a supply. But as a general rule, we choose vodka for Bottle #1—it's the best-selling liquor in the country and it's versatile, so you can serve it on the rocks or mix it with any kind of juice, soda, or tonic. For Bottle #2, we choose by season: If it's spring or summer, we supply another white liquor, either gin or rum. If it's fall or winter, we go with a brown liquor—generally Scotch or bourbon.

HOW MANY DRINKS TO PROVIDE: THE COCKTAIL CALCULATOR

Our guidelines for figuring out how many drinks we'll need are fairly liberal since it's always better to have liquor left over than to suddenly run dry mid-party. We also assume our party will last at least four hours and maybe more, but if you're keeping your event to a defined two-hour time slot, adjust accordingly.

STEP 1: CALCULATE THE TOTAL NUMBER OF DRINKS YOU'LL NEED

These numbers are based on years of keeping track of how much alcohol we go through at any given party. Obviously, you'll have some people who'll drink more cocktails than you allot, but they're made up for by those who nurse a single drink all evening. The calculations below should help you have enough for everybody:

Signature cocktails: plan on 2½ drinks per person

Additional liquor (on the bar): plan on ½ drink per person

Additional wine or beer: plan on 1½ drinks per person

step 2: calculate how much liquor that requires you to provide

Signature cocktails: Many of our signature cocktail recipes can be made by the pitcher, which is about 20 drinks. The pitcher recipes are expressed in cups to make measuring easier. For every 3 cups of liquor you need, buy one 750-milliliter bottle.

Additional liquor: One 750-milliliter bottle provides 12 to 15 drinks. If you have 30 or fewer people at your party, you need just one bottle each of your two additional liquors.

Additional wine or beer: One bottle of wine provides about 6 drinks; one bottle of beer counts as one drink. Our crowd tends to have far more wine drinkers than beer fans, so we go heavier on the vino.

Mixers/nonalcoholic drinks: In addition to the ingredients you need for your signature cocktail, buy mixers (tonic, club soda, cola, diet cola, etc.) that will be used both for cocktails and by guests who want a nonalcoholic alternative. For a party of 20 or fewer of people, provide 1 liter of each mixer. For a party of more than 20, supply 2 liters. Also, always have plenty of water available.

HOW TO MAKE DRINKS BY THE PITCHER: THE COCKTAIL CONVERTER

Mixing the signature cocktails in large amounts keeps you from being stuck behind the bar all night, so throughout the book we've given you the recipe for a pitcher's worth where appropriate (some drinks don't lend themselves to pre-mixing). Of course, you may have a favorite cocktail of your own that you'd like to feature, so to help you easily multiply any single-drink recipe, we've created this handy conversion chart.

If a one-drink recipe calls for:	Make a pitcher (about 20 drinks) by using:
¼ ounce	½ cup + 2 tablespoons
½ ounce	1¼ cups
¾ ounce	1¾ cups + 2 tablespoons
1 ounce	2½ cups
1½ ounces	3¾ cups
2 ounces	5 cups
1 teaspoon	¼ cup plus 3 scant tablespoons
dash (of bitters, for instance)	2½ teaspoons

A couple of tips to remember when you're mixing drinks by the pitcher:

- Always add carbonated ingredients like club soda or ginger ale to the individual drinks, rather than to the entire pitcher, to preserve the fizz.

- Some recipes direct you to shake the cocktail with ice rather than just stir the ingredients together. This slightly dilutes the drink, which makes a difference in both taste and strength. When you're making a pitcher of a shaken cocktail, add several handfuls of ice cubes to the pitcher and stir vigorously to promote melting. When the cubes are about half their original size, spoon them out and discard.

ESSENTIAL ELEMENT #3
THE GUESTS

We know professional party planners in New York City who are paid thousands of dollars to compile guest lists full of Fabulous People—the idea being that a party's success relies, in the end, on who attends. Oooh, there's Minor Celebrity over by the bar! Hey, isn't that Important Politician just walking in?

Of course, we agree that you have to give some thought to your guest list, and especially to how many people to invite (which we've always thought was the knottier problem). We give you some guidelines about that below. But we believe that what makes a party truly fun isn't who your invitees are so much as that certain festive energy that arises when everyone has loosened up and let the party spirit take over. Our Conversation Kick-Starters, which you'll find at the start of each party, will help you make that happen every time. They'll guarantee that your guests clamor to be invited to your next party.

GETTING THE RIGHT GROUP OF PEOPLE TO YOUR PARTY: GUEST-LIST GUIDELINES

The number of people you invite to your cocktail party depends on lots of factors: how big your home is, how much cooking you have time for, how many friends will be disappointed if they're not included. But all those considerations aside, it helps to start with some upper and lower limits, so over the years, we've developed a couple of helpful how-many-to-invite parameters.

Our target number of guests for a cocktail party is 25, and we try to stay within 10 on either side of that. More than 35, and the prep work gets out of hand and we're too exhausted to enjoy ourselves. Fewer than 15, and the event begins to feel a bit sedate—more like a dinner party than a cocktail party. A crowd of 25 feels festive and increases every guest's chances of encountering some interesting person he hasn't met before.

Another way to think about how big the party should be is to visualize how the guests will fill out your home. As a rough rule of thumb, use our Guests-to-Seats Ratio: Count all the places guests could sit in the main area of your home—not just the usual suspects like sofas and chairs, but also places people might perch. (At our parties, someone always sits on the ottoman, and our windowsills are wide, so two people can prop themselves there.) Now multiply. Aim to have about three people for every seat. When the majority of people are standing, a party takes on a lovely swirly, mingly atmosphere. Too many sitters, and you're back in dinner-party land. Not a bad thing, but not what you're after.

Once you've got a target number, you have to figure out how many people to invite to get that ideal number to show up. Here, too, the guidelines are rough, but we generally plan for a 70 percent acceptance rate. So to get 25 people at our party, we invite somewhere around 36. Keep in mind that this number will fluctuate. In our party notebook, we've recorded acceptance rates as low as 56 percent and as high as 87 percent. (For more about the notebook, see page 166.)

Finally, a word on creating a good mix of people. This isn't something to agonize over—you're not the recreation director at Club Med, after all. But it is worth a little bit of thought. We like to make an off-the-top-of-our-heads list that simply includes people we like. Then we go back over it with an eye toward variety: If there are tons of couples, we try to include a few more single people; if the crowd is mostly friends from work, we try to mix in old college pals. And we try to keep the male-female ratio fairly even. In the end, though, the most essential characteristic of the guests is that they're people we look forward to hanging out with.

GUARANTEEING YOUR GUESTS' GOOD TIME: CONVERSATION KICK-STARTERS

Think about the best cocktail party you ever attended: You floated from conversation to conversation. There were no awkward pauses, no boring chit-chat about the weather. You seemed to effortlessly meet everyone in the room. Time flew by—how did it get to be midnight already?—and you left feeling fortunate that you'd been invited. The true mark of a successful cocktail party is that hard-to-define but easy-to-recognize camaraderie that develops among the guests, that "aren't we all lucky to be here" atmosphere that makes the night feel special.

To guarantee that magic at every single occasion, we created our unique Conversation Kick-Starters, which get guests mingling without even noticing that they're doing it. You'll find one in each party chapter: At the Make-Your-Own Martini Party, for instance, guests are invited to mix the signature cocktails themselves—or come up with their own. Instead of searching awkwardly for opening gambits (So, what do you do? How do you know the host?), they're quickly asking each other to pass the pear brandy or wondering aloud whether a blue drink could possibly taste good. At our "Map-Happy Evening," we take advantage of the fact that everyone loves to travel—and to talk about where they've been—by putting up a giant world map and supplying plenty of pushpins. Guests can't resist gathering around the map, and conversations crop up easily. Each of our Kick-Starters creates a natural, relaxed way for guests to meet one another; there are no contrived party games or silly costumes here, just smart, stylish opportunities for interaction. The result: Every guest leaves at the end of the night with that "what a great party" glow.

The fINAL TOUCH
SISTERS' SECRETS TO CONfIDENT HOSTESSING

You've got a menu, a signature cocktail, a guest list, a party date, and if you're like most hosts, perhaps a few remaining worries: Will I get everything done in time? What if I run out of food? How do I make sure I get to greet all my guests? To help you master the art of gracious entertaining—and keep you calm and confident throughout the planning and the party itself—we've supplied you with our Sisters' Secrets to Confident Hostessing. They're our most helpful, down-to-earth shortcuts and tricks, the sort of nitty-gritty info and practical problem-solving advice that we share with each other and our closest friends. . . and now you. You'll find the secrets sprinkled throughout the book, but if you've got a burning party question *right now*, here's where you'll find the answer:

fOOD

DRINKS

GUESTS

ATMOSPHERE

PLANNING

THE
PARTIES

A MAP-HAPPY EVENING
For Anyone who's Been Anywhere

We used to have a *New Yorker* cartoon taped to our refrigerator that showed two guys talking. "Travel," one said to the other, "is the sherbet between courses of reality." We've seen dull conversations about insurance rates or the new lawnmower models at Home Depot suddenly liven up when someone says, "You know, I just got back from a trip to India". . . or Rio or Napa Valley. Everyone has a tourist tale he loves to share, whether it's the mother of all luggage disasters or a triumphant we-just-happened-upon-it discovery. All you need for this party are an oversized world map and plenty of pushpins to tempt guests to "mark their spots." Instead of lamely asking each other "So, where are you from?" they'll be exclaiming "Wow, you've been *there?*"

CONVERSATION
KICK-STARTER

The gist: You hang a large world map in a prominent place in the room and next to it, place a bowl of pushpins and a card that says, "Where in the world have you been? Please mark the two or three most interesting places you've traveled." As guests push in their pins and look to see where other people have been, it creates countless opportunities to swap stories, compare notes with others who've been to the same places, or even ask for travel recommendations.

The logistics: Use as big a map as you can find so that the largest number of people can gather around it at once. We bought ours at Barnes & Noble for around eight dollars and used spray adhesive to stick it to a piece of foamboard we picked up at an office-supply store. If you're pressed for time, you can tape a map to the wall and let guests use colored pens instead of thumbtacks, but it's worth it to go the foamboard route—pushing in the pins gives a satisfying Situation Room effect.

As with all the Conversation Kick-Starters in this book, there's no need to make a big production out of the fact that the map is there. Prime your guests by mentioning maps or travel on the invitations you send out (use our party name or create one of your own), then just place the map somewhere central and let the party-goers discover it on their own. There's usually a snowball effect: One or two guests get involved with the map, another wanders over to see what they're doing, they start talking and perusing the map together, which attracts more people . . . and so on. And conversations continue throughout the party, not just map-side: When our friend Jen came to one of our Map-Happy parties, she was considering a trip to Australia and thought she might meet other people who'd been there. Sure enough, when she made her way over to the map, there was a pin stuck squarely in Sydney. Jen began trying to figure out who had put it there. First, she asked a very cute lawyer who was standing near the bar if he was the "Australia Guy." He wasn't, but they struck up a conversation about Spain, where they'd both traveled. Next, she asked a nice-looking man near the hors d'oeuvres table if *he* was the Australia Guy. Nope, he'd put his pins in Alaska and Nepal, but Australia was on his destination dream list and they talked for a while about other places they wanted to visit.

And so it went. Jen told us the next day that she never actually figured out who had put that pin in Australia, but she'd met at least six new people—and had a date with Alaska Guy the next weekend.

A simple trick to make each guest feel special

What's your mental image of a gracious hostess? We picture someone gliding effortlessly around a party, sprinkling warm introductions and clever conversational tidbits over her guests like magic fairy dust, artfully but unobtrusively drawing them into the mood and mix of the party. (This can apply to men, too, of course, though when we picture a gracious host, he's more likely to toss the fairy dust in handfuls than to sprinkle it.)

Simply put, the art of hostessing lies in making each guest feel special. A big responsibility, sure, but easier to accomplish than you might think. In fact, we've discovered one very simple secret weapon that will transform you from garden-variety party-giver to hostess extraordinaire. It isn't actually magic fairy dust, but it works just as well: It's a tray of hors d'oeuvres.

Sound odd? Well, think about how a party typically goes for the host: You greet everyone at the door, point them toward the bar, and once the party is pretty much under way, begin circulating through the room. And that's where you get trapped. Everyone wants to have a conversation with you, but 15 minutes each with 20 guests is 5 hours' worth of conversation. You don't have that kind of time! With a tray of tasty hors d'oeuvres in hand, you can:

. . . give every guest a little personal attention—for a minute or two. Your hors d'oeuvre tray is a built-in excuse to keep moving from group to group. "Oh, I'd love to hear more about your honeymoon/kids/liposuction," you say. "Let me make sure everyone gets a chance at these cheese puffs and then I want to get the whole story." Move to the next group. Repeat as needed.

. . . make sure everybody mingles. Guests will gravitate to you and your tray, which not only helps redistribute all those little conversational groups but also gives you lots of natural opportunities to introduce people as they take a tidbit.

. . . help shy types get into the swing of things. If you spot a guest on the sidelines, put the magical tray in his or her hands. It's like a coat of protective party armor, allowing her to approach anyone and everyone without awkwardness.

WHEN YOU *want to keep a party moving, serve a festive drink with a wanderlust theme. We found the Border Crossing, a retro tequila cocktail, in a 1971 bartending book and tinkered with it a bit to bring it up to date. (Extensive cocktail testing is part of the job—tough assignment, right?) We're not big sticklers about glassware rules: We serve almost all of our cocktails in short cocktail glasses (sometimes referred to as old-fashioned or rocks glasses).*

BORDER CROSSING

TO MAKE ONE DRINK:

> 1½ ounces tequila
>
> ½ ounce raspberry liqueur (such as Chambord)
>
> ½ ounce fresh lime juice
>
> 1 teaspoon superfine sugar

SHAKE all the ingredients with ice and strain into an ice-filled glass.

In the "How to Get Organized" chapter, we explained the advantages of making your signature cocktails by the pitcher. Wherever appropriate, we've given you the recipe for one drink and for 20 (the amount that fits in most large pitchers). Use the Cocktail Converter on page 12 to make a pitcher of drinks from your own recipes.

TO MAKE A PITCHER (ABOUT 20 DRINKS):

> 3¾ cups tequila
>
> 1¼ cups raspberry liqueur (such as Chambord)
>
> 1¼ cups fresh lime juice
>
> ¼ cup plus 3 scant tablespoons superfine sugar

COMBINE all the ingredients in a large pitcher, add ice, and stir for about 30 seconds. Spoon out the ice cubes. Store the pitcher in the refrigerator until party time.

THE MENU

"International" foods

Moroccan Lamb Meatballs with Dill Sauce

Mexican Black Bean Quesadillas

Italian Baked Ravioli

Crudités with Indian Curry Dip

Greek Olives

Recipes

moroccan lamb meatballs with dill sauce

MAKES ABOUT 32 MEATBALLS

We adapted this recipe from a favorite food magazine, and when we say "adapted" we always, *always* mean "made it simpler." These have been a crowd-pleaser at Purcell parties for years—so much so that when we don't serve them, guests actually complain.

FOR THE MEATBALLS

$^1/_3$ cup minced onion

1 garlic clove, minced

$1^1/_2$ teaspoons olive oil

1 teaspoon salt

$^1/_2$ teaspoon dried mint, crumbled

$^1/_2$ teaspoon ground allspice

$^1/_4$ teaspoon ground cinnamon

1 pound ground lamb

1 cup fine fresh bread crumbs (about 2 slices white bread, ground in food processor)

1 egg, lightly beaten

$^1/_4$ cup white sesame seeds

2 tablespoons finely chopped cranberries

FOR THE SAUCE

$^1/_2$ cup mayonnaise

$^1/_2$ cup sour cream

$^1/_4$ cup chopped fresh dill

2 garlic cloves, minced

$1^1/_2$ teaspoons Dijon mustard

$^1/_2$ teaspoon lemon juice

$^1/_4$ teaspoon salt

ground white pepper to taste*

---

* *Don't you hate those little asterisks in recipes? You just know they're going to say something like "You can buy this ingredient in out-of-the-way Asian markets or mail order it for enormous sums and wait three weeks for it to arrive." But not in our recipes. Behind every asterisk, you'll find some shortcut or explanation that will make your life easier. We promise. In this case, a word about white pepper. We use white instead of black pepper because it doesn't leave black flecks in the sauce, but there's no real taste difference, so you don't have to run out to buy white pepper if you don't already have it.*

PREHEAT oven to 450°F.

PREPARE the meatballs: In a small, nonstick skillet, cook the onion and garlic in the olive oil over moderately low heat, stirring, until softened but not browned, 8 to 10 minutes. Scrape the mixture into a big bowl and stir in the salt, mint, allspice, and cinnamon. Add the lamb, bread crumbs, egg, sesame seeds, and currants and combine thoroughly (the easiest way is to use your hands). Roll the mixture into 1¼-inch balls. (Guests will be spearing them with toothpicks, so they should be no bigger than two bites' worth.) Line up the meatballs on an ungreased baking sheet as you go (they can be close, just not touching).

BAKE just until no longer pink in the middle, 8 to 10 minutes.

PREPARE the sauce: Mix all the ingredients in the bowl in which you plan to serve the sauce (why not save yourself the extra dishwashing?). Run a clean finger or a damp paper towel around the inside rim to make it neat and pretty.

WHEN ready to serve, transfer the meatballs to a serving platter, warm or at room temperature. Serve the sauce alongside.

make-ahead factor: *The dill sauce can be made 3 to 4 days ahead and kept covered and refrigerated. The meatballs can be formed 1 day ahead and kept covered and refrigerated until ready to bake.*

SISTERS' SECRETS TO CONFIDENT HOSTESSING
The easy way to create a party soundtrack

Music gives a party momentum, but if you don't have hours to spare to create your own perfect mix, don't worry. Just buy four or five pre-mixed CDs from the now seemingly innumerable clothing stores, coffee shops, and home emporiums that sell them. We've found all-jazz CDs, Latin music mixes, even collections with names like "Martini Madness" or "Cocktail Classics" that almost beg to be played at a real party instead of over a store P.A. system. Sure, it's enough to make a true music buff hang her head in shame, but remember, this is background music. Those retail giants pay huge bucks to researchers to create an inviting atmosphere in their stores. Why not let your party benefit from that expertise?

mexican black bean quesadillas

MAKES ABOUT 60 QUESADILLA WEDGES

We have a lot of vegetarian friends, so we always try to make at least one meatless hors d'oeuvre. This one is equally popular with carnivores. Add a little more minced jalapeño to take it from subtly spicy to downright fiery.

2 (15-ounce) cans black beans, drained

6 scallions, finely chopped (white and pale green parts)

1/2 cup seeded and finely chopped red bell pepper

1/4 cup chopped fresh cilantro*

2 large garlic cloves, minced

1 1/2 tablespoons seeded and minced jalapeño pepper

3 teaspoons ground cumin

salt and pepper

1 egg, lightly beaten

2 to 4 tablespoons yellow cornmeal**

2 packages fajita-sized (7 1/2-inch) flour tortillas (20 to 24 tortillas total)

olive oil for brushing on tortillas

8 ounces sour cream

juice of 1 lime

IN A LARGE BOWL, coarsely mash the drained beans with a hand masher or the back of a big spoon. Add the scallions, bell pepper, cilantro, garlic, jalapeño pepper, and 2 teaspoons of the cumin; mix well. Add salt and pepper to taste. Stir in the egg and cornmeal.

SPREAD bean mixture in a 1/4-inch layer between two tortillas to form one quesadilla. Brush both sides of the quesadilla with olive oil. Repeat with the rest of the tortillas. Brown each quesadilla in a skillet over medium heat, pressing it down (a small pan lid works well), so it browns evenly. Cut each quesadilla into six wedges, pizza-style.

MIX the remaining 1 teaspoon cumin into the sour cream and add a squeeze of lime juice or more to taste. Serve alongside the quesadilla wedges.

make-ahead factor: *The quesadilla wedges can be made up to 2 days ahead and kept covered and refrigerated. Warm them in a 400°F oven until crispy, about 10 minutes.*

---

* *Cilantro is a classic herb in Mexican dishes. If, like Anne, you think it tastes like dishwashing detergent, it's fine to skip it.*

** *Cornmeal makes the mixture thicker, so it's less likely to squirt out from between the tortillas when guests bite into the quesadillas. Don't leave it out.*

italian baked ravioli

Someone once gave us a pasta machine. We're pretty sure it's in its original box in a closet somewhere. Sure, some things taste better made from scratch, but we're always on the lookout for smart shortcuts that aren't a flavor compromise, and pre-made refrigerated ravioli is one of them.

1 (5-ounce) package small fresh cheese ravioli*

2 eggs

3/4 cup dry bread crumbs

2 tablespoons grated Parmesan cheese

1 teaspoon dried basil

1 teaspoon dried oregano

1/4 teaspoon pepper

purchased marinara sauce for dipping

PREHEAT oven to 375°F. Coat a baking sheet with cooking spray.

BOIL THE RAVIOLI according to the package instructions. Drain in a colander and let cool to room temperature.

WHILE RAVIOLI ARE COOKING, beat the eggs lightly. In a separate bowl, combine the bread crumbs, Parmesan cheese, basil, oregano, and pepper. Dip each of the ravioli in the egg, then the crumb mixture, coating all sides. Arrange the ravioli on the baking sheet. Bake until crisp, 12 to 14 minutes. The ravioli will puff up slightly and turn golden brown. Serve them with the marinara sauce.

make-ahead factor: *The ravioli can be breaded 1 day ahead and kept covered and refrigerated until ready to bake.*

* *You'll find fresh ravioli in the refrigerated section of the supermarket. Don't be tempted to substitute meat-filled ravioli, especially if you're going to make these ahead of time. They don't hold up nearly as well as the cheese variety.*

crudités with indian curry dip

MAKES APPROXIMATELY (VERY APPROXIMATELY!) 100 PIECES AND ABOUT 1½ CUPS OF DIP

Bland, boring broccoli florets and carrot sticks have given crudités a bad rap. But when you serve crudités with interesting flavors, colors, and shapes and a scrumptious dip, your guests will devour them. Our mom turned us on to this dip. She found the original recipe in a *Southern Living Party Cookbook* that's almost as old as we are. Good recipes survive forever!

FOR THE CRUDITÉS

1 red bell pepper

1 yellow bell pepper

1 orange bell pepper

1 hothouse (seedless) cucumber

20 to 30 asparagus spears

20 to 30 snow peas

FOR THE DIP

1 cup sour cream

½ cup mayonnaise

2 tablespoons minced fresh parsley

2 tablespoons grated onion

1 tablespoon minced chives

1 tablespoon lemon juice

2 teaspoons Dijon mustard

1 teaspoon mild curry powder

½ teaspoon dried tarragon, crushed

½ teaspoon paprika

3 dashes Tabasco sauce, or to taste

salt and pepper

PREPARE THE CRUDITÉS: Quarter the peppers and remove the core, seeds, and ribs. Cut each quarter in half diagonally so you have two triangles, each with a curved base.

SCORE THE CUCUMBER lengthwise with the tines of a fork to remove strips of skin, creating stripes. Cut the cucumber crosswise in half or in thirds, depending on how long it is, to make 4- to 5-inch-long sections, then cut each section lengthwise into slim wedges.

BLANCH THE ASPARAGUS spears and the snow peas at the same time: Drop them into a pot of generously salted, boiling water and cook until you can pierce the asparagus spears with a fork but they're still crisp, 3 to 5 minutes depending on the thickness of the spears. (The snow peas are more forgiving, so focus on whether the asparagus spears are done.) Immediately plunge the vegetables into a bowl of ice water until they're no longer warm. Pat dry with paper towels.

PREPARE THE DIP: Mix all the ingredients together in a bowl. Add salt and pepper to taste.

TO MAKE AN APPEALING DISPLAY, serve the vegetables standing up in a bowl instead of laying them flat on a plate or tray.

make-ahead factor: *All the vegetables can be cut and blanched (if necessary) 1 day ahead. Keep them in the refrigerator loosely wrapped in damp paper towels. The dip can be made 3 to 4 days ahead and kept covered and refrigerated.*

greek olives

Buy fresh Greek olives at the grocery store and mound them into bowls around your party space. Don't forget to provide smaller bowls to discard the pits, and place a pit (a neat one—no hunks of olive flesh) in each one to give guests the idea.

ANY EXCUSE TO CELEBRATE!

Just about any occasion calls for a celebration if you're in a party-throwing mood—and we always are! Why wait for the next birthday or anniversary? Throw this party to celebrate teeny triumphs and small successes— landed a new job? adopted a kitten? scored a serious bargain at a sample sale? Get all the guests in on the act by having them share their own excuses to celebrate, major or minor. At our parties, guests have celebrated everything from getting engaged to "persuading dad to get rid of his comb-over." The brilliance of this party is that there isn't just one birthday girl or guest of honor; *everybody* has a special reason to feel festive.

Conversation
Kick-Starter

The gist: As guests arrive, each jots down a personal "excuse to celebrate" on a strip of paper and fastens it around the stem of a Champagne flute (in which the signature cocktails are served). The sometimes sweet, sometimes hilarious reasons party-goers give for celebrating provide a neatly built-in conversation-starter. Before you know it, everyone is checking out one another's "excuses," clinking glasses and chatting easily.

The logistics: When you send out invitations, give your guests a heads-up on the theme of the party by including the words "Everybody celebrate!" along with a clue about what you, the host, are celebrating, and the words "Please come prepared to share your own reason to celebrate—irreverence encouraged."

Make strips out of any light-colored, fairly heavyweight paper (we like vellum, which looks elegant, but be sure that your pens will write on its fairly slick surface without smudging). Cut strips about ½ inch wide and 11 inches long. Color in a 4-inch section at the end of each strip so guests don't use that space to write—it won't be readable once the strip is wrapped around the flute stem. Provide tape for guests to attach the strips around the stems of their glasses or cut small slits near the end of each strip to thread the opposite end through.

Create an example excuse, thread it around the stem of a Champagne flute, and put the flute on a table or window sill with more paper strips and plenty of pens. As you greet arriving guests, direct them to the table to write down their celebration excuses. Create enough strips for all your party guests plus plenty of extras: Some guests won't want to stop at one. You'll find that as the cocktails flow, so does the creativity!

Three smart ways to chill champagne or wine

Obviously, you need to have lots of cold Champagne on hand for this party. Do not, as we once did, wait until the last minute and then chill the Champagne in the freezer. You will get distracted; you will leave the Champagne in too long; you will hear with a sinking sensation in your gut the muffled sound of a bottle exploding (we were still finding glass shards months later). Please, we beg you, try these other options, all of which apply to white wine, as well.

If you have loads of room in the refrigerator: Put the bottles in to chill at least 3 hours before party time. The coldest place in the fridge is on the bottom shelf toward the back; avoid putting bottles in the door, which is the warmest area.

If you have counter space to spare: Use the multi-ice-bucket method. Any deep container—large mixing bowls or small, clean wastebaskets—can substitute. Place a bottle in each bucket, then add as many ice cubes as will fit and fill with water. The Champagne or wine will be chilled in about 20 minutes. If you have coarse salt on hand, add about 1 cup for every 5 cups of ice—it slightly speeds up the chilling process (it has to do with lowering the melting point of the ice—you'll just have to trust us on the science).

If your kitchen's tiny: Put your tub to use. Manhattan kitchens are minuscule, so this is our preferred method: Chill all the bottles at once in a couple of cheap Styrofoam coolers you can pick up at the grocery store for about two dollars apiece. The coolers tend to leak, so stand them in the bathtub. Load them up with the bottles about half an hour before party time, then fill with ice and water. Voilà! Instant wet bar.

WHAT KIND *of cocktails does a celebration call for? Champagne cocktails, of course! Two of our absolute favorites are the Nelson's Blood, named partly for its seductive red color, and the sophisticated, citrusy French 75. For maximum fizz with minimum fuss, set out your Champagne flutes already containing all the cocktail ingredients except the bubbly, which guests add themselves as they pick up a glass. Create a little card with the name of the drink. Include the recipe, so guests can mix their next drink on their own.*

NELSON'S BLOOD

TO MAKE ONE DRINK:

> ¹/₂ **ounce tawny port**
> **Champagne**

POUR the port into a Champagne flute. Top off with Champagne.

FRENCH 75

TO MAKE ONE DRINK:

> ¹/₂ **ounce gin**
> ¹/₂ **ounce fresh lemon juice**
> ¹/₂ **teaspoon superfine sugar**
> **Champagne**

POUR the gin and lemon juice into a Champagne flute and stir in the superfine sugar until dissolved (one of those disposable wooden chopsticks you get with Chinese takeout works great for this). Top off with Champagne.

THE MENU

Elegant finger foods that signal a celebration

Beef Tenderloin and Pearl Onion Skewers

Wild Mushroom Tartlets

Smoked Trout Spread

Asparagus Spears with Lemon Dipping Sauce

Lemon-Glazed Pecans

SISTERS' SECRETS TO CONFIDENT HOSTESSING

How to throw a champagne party on a beer budget

We're well aware that officially, Champagne refers only to the drink made in the Champagne region of France, and believe us, we never turn down a glass of the scrumptious stuff. But if your budget for bubbly doesn't cover the "real thing," do as we frequently do: Substitute sparkling wine, which is generally less expensive (we've had particular luck finding good Spanish cavas for under $15). No matter whether you go French or faux, be sure to buy sparklers labeled brut or extra brut, or your cocktails will taste too sweet. And remember: It's worth asking for a discount if you're buying in bulk. Most wine stores take 10 percent off when you buy a full case.

Recipes

beef tenderloin and pearl onion skewers

MAKES ABOUT 50 SKEWERS

Recipes for skewered foods usually instruct you to broil the already-assembled skewers, turning each one individually to ensure even cooking. We adapted this one so that you cook the unskewered cubes in a skillet, which allows you to easily flip them with a spatula. Plus, if you run out of time before the party, you can always just put out the beef cubes, the onions, and a pile of skewers and encourage guests to assemble the hors d'oeuvres themselves.

FOR THE ONIONS

1 (10-ounce) bottle cocktail onions

1 tablespoon butter

salt and pepper

FOR THE BEEF TENDERLOIN

1 pound beef tenderloin, cut into $^3/_4$-inch cubes

2 garlic cloves, minced

$1^1/_2$ teaspoons finely chopped fresh rosemary

1 teaspoon coarse salt

$^1/_2$ teaspoon coarsely ground black pepper

2 to 3 tablespoons olive oil

PREPARE THE ONIONS: Drain the cocktail onions and soak them in a large bowl filled with cold water for about 1 hour. Change the water and soak for another hour. (This tones down the intense vinegar flavor just a bit.) Melt the butter in a large skillet over medium heat. Add the onions and cook, stirring, about 4 minutes (the onions may lightly brown—that's fine). Add salt and pepper to taste. Remove from heat.

PREPARE THE BEEF: Put the tenderloin cubes, garlic, rosemary, salt, and pepper in a resealable plastic bag and gently shake until cubes are coated. Heat the olive oil in a large skillet over high heat. When the oil is hot, add the beef and sear until the outsides of the cubes are brown and insides are still rare, 3 to 5 minutes. Remove from heat.

PUT ONE ONION, then one beef tenderloin cube on each skewer or toothpick, so the hors d'oeuvres will stand up on a platter, each skewer sticking out the top. Serve warm. (See "How to keep warm foods warm" on page 57.)

make-ahead factor: *The skewers can be prepared 1 day ahead and kept covered and refrigerated. Warm them in a 300°F oven for 4 to 6 minutes. (They don't need to be piping-hot; just take the chill off. Heat them any more and you risk overcooking the beef.)*

wild mushroom tartlets

MAKES 48 TARTLETS

These impressive-looking tartlets are a cinch to make and they fly off the tray as fast as you can serve them. Even Lauren, who's a lifelong mushroom avoider, can't resist them. Don't be put off by the idea of making your own tart crusts. This dough is extremely easy to work with and no kneading or rolling out is required.

FOR THE CRUST

8 ounces cream cheese, softened

4 tablespoons ($\frac{1}{2}$ stick) butter, softened

$1\frac{1}{2}$ cups all-purpose flour

$\frac{1}{4}$ teaspoon salt

FOR THE FILLING

2 tablespoons butter

16 ounces mixed wild mushrooms (roughly 7 cups), finely chopped*

1 cup chopped scallions (white and pale green parts)

4 tablespoons balsamic vinegar

2 eggs, lightly beaten

2 teaspoons all-purpose flour

$\frac{1}{2}$ teaspoon dried thyme

$\frac{1}{4}$ teaspoon salt

$\frac{1}{2}$ cup shredded Swiss cheese

$\frac{1}{4}$ cup grated Parmesan cheese

PREPARE THE CRUST: Beat the cream cheese and butter with an electric mixer until smooth. Add the flour and salt and mix until well blended. Form the mixture into a ball, cover, and chill for 1 hour or overnight.

PREHEAT oven to 375°F.

PREPARE THE FILLING: In a large saucepan, melt the butter over medium heat. Add the mushrooms and scallions, and cook until the mushrooms are tender, 5 to 10 minutes. Drain off any excess liquid, then add the balsamic vinegar and stir thoroughly. Cook for 1 more minute. Let the mixture cool slightly.

IN A LARGE BOWL, mix the eggs, flour, thyme, and salt with a spoon. Stir the cheeses into the egg mixture, then stir in the mushrooms.

* *We use cremini, white, shiitake, and portobello mushrooms, but if all you can find are white, these tartlets will still be delicious. Remember with shiitakes to remove the tough stems before you chop them.*

DIVIDE the chilled dough into 48 pieces. Press each piece into the cup of an ungreased miniature muffin tin so it covers the bottom and the sides. This does not have to be a precise operation—the dough puffs a bit when baked and is surprisingly sturdy, so don't worry if there are thin spots when you press it into the muffin cups. Spoon the mushroom mixture into the cups so it's level with the top of each cup. Bake until the tart crusts are puffed and golden brown, 15 to 20 minutes.

make-ahead factor: *The dough can be made up to 2 days ahead and kept covered and refrigerated. The cooked tartlets can be refrigerated for 1 day or frozen for up to 2 weeks. Warm them in a 300°F oven for 10 to 15 minutes if tarts were refrigerated, 20 to 25 if frozen.*

smoked trout spread

P art of the appeal of this rich dip is that it's super-quick to make, but beware: It's also super-quick to disappear. We once caught a party guest pawing through the fridge to find more!

1 pound smoked trout*	**2 tablespoons minced onion**
1 cup mayonnaise	**1 teaspoon lemon zest**
1 cup sour cream	**pinch cayenne**
4 tablespoons chopped fresh dill	**salt**
4 tablespoons drained prepared horseradish	

DISCARD the skin and any bones from the trout. Break the fish into pieces and pulse in the food processor until finely chopped (but not pureed). Transfer to a bowl; stir in the rest of the ingredients and add salt to taste.

NO EFFORT: Serve with crackers.

LOW EFFORT: Along with the crackers, serve ¼-inch-thick slices of hothouse (seedless) cucumber.

MO' EFFORT: Add a third accompaniment: thin slices of Granny Smith apple. Toss the slices in lemon juice immediately after cutting to keep them from turning brown.

make-ahead factor: *The trout dip can be made 2 days ahead and kept covered and refrigerated. The cucumber can be sliced, wrapped in damp paper towels, and kept in a resealable plastic bag in the refrigerator for 1 day.*

---

* *Look for smoked trout fillets in the deli section (they're packaged in plastic, much like bacon). Smoked mullet or mackerel can be substituted.*

asparagus spears with lemon dipping sauce

MAKES 40 TO 50 ASPARAGUS SPEARS AND ABOUT 1 CUP OF DIP

We once went all-out and made Hollandaise sauce to serve with asparagus spears. Major pain in the neck! In our never-ending quest to make things easier and more do-aheadable, we created this lemony sauce that's just as tasty, takes two minutes to mix, and keeps in the fridge for days.

2 pounds medium asparagus (40 to 50 spears)

FOR THE DIPPING SAUCE

³/₄ cup sour cream

¹/₄ cup mayonnaise

2 tablespoons lemon juice

1¹/₂ tablespoons minced parsley

1 tablespoon Dijon mustard

2 teaspoons grated lemon zest

1 garlic clove, finely minced

salt and pepper

PREPARE THE ASPARAGUS: Snap off the tough ends of the asparagus spears and blanch them by dropping them into a pot of generously salted, boiling water. Cook until you can pierce them with a fork but they're still crisp, 3 to 5 minutes depending on the thickness of the spears. Immediately plunge them into a bowl of ice water until no longer warm. Pat dry with paper towels and chill in the refrigerator.

PREPARE THE DIPPING SAUCE: Mix all the ingredients in a small bowl. Add salt and pepper to taste.

ARRANGE the asparagus standing up in pretty drinking glasses and serve the sauce alongside.

make-ahead factor: *The asparagus can be blanched 1 day ahead and kept refrigerated, loosely wrapped in damp paper towels. The sauce can be made 3 to 4 days ahead and kept covered and refrigerated.*

lemon-glazed pecans

MAKES ABOUT 4 CUPS OF NUTS

We have more than 20 recipes for jazzed-up nuts in our collection and these unusual, sweet-but-not-too-sweet pecans always inspire compliments. We've seen similar recipes that use much more cinnamon, or ground ginger in place of the nutmeg. Taste your sugar mix before you coat the nuts and adjust the spices however you like. Serve the nuts in bowls around the room.

1 cup sugar

2 tablespoons grated lemon peel
(from 2 to 3 lemons)

1 teaspoon ground cinnamon

1/2 teaspoon grated nutmeg

1/2 teaspoon salt

2 egg whites

2 teaspoons fresh lemon juice

1 pound pecan halves

PREHEAT oven to 250°F. Line two baking sheets with parchment paper.*

IN A LARGE BOWL, mix the sugar, lemon peel, cinnamon, nutmeg, and salt and set aside.

IN ANOTHER LARGE BOWL, whisk the egg whites and lemon juice until foamy, about 1 minute. Add the pecans and toss until they're lightly coated. Drain off any excess liquid.

ADD the nuts to the sugar mixture, tossing until nuts are evenly coated. Spread the nuts on the parchment-lined baking sheets, removing any loose clumps of sugar. Bake 20 minutes. Stir the nuts and rotate the baking sheets so the one on the top rack moves to the bottom, and vice versa. Bake until the nuts are golden and dry, an additional 20 to 25 minutes.

TO prevent the nuts from sticking to one another, let them cool completely on the baking sheets before you transfer them to bowls.

make-ahead factor: *The nuts can be made up to 2 weeks ahead and kept tightly covered.*

---

* *Parchment paper is a must. If you use aluminum foil instead, as we once did, you'll find yourself scraping little bits of foil off of each nut. In a pinch, you can use sheets cut from brown paper bags.*

APHRODITE'S DELIGHT
eat and drink to your heart's content

Are there really foods that stoke sexual desire? Who knows, but there's definitely a cocktail party that seduces guests' senses, and this is it. Delectable nibbles and naughtily named cocktails loosen up everyone's mood and entice guests into mingling easily with their fellow party-goers.

Conversation
KICK-STARTER

The gist: This party's signature cocktail is the Between the Sheets—and its name gives guests a crucial clue to the mingle-encouraging activity awaiting them. It all starts with several bowls filled with Ping-Pong balls. Don't ask us to explain their appeal; all we know is that people can't resist picking them up (and juggling them and tossing them across the room to each other). And when they do, they discover that each one is inked with a hypothetical Between-the-Sheets pairing. Who would you opt to canoodle with if you absolutely had to choose: Hillary Clinton or Martha Stewart? Ginger or Mary Ann? Paul Newman or Robert Redford? Once they've run through one bowlful of balls, you'll find groups of guests eagerly migrating over to the next bowl to continue the fun.

The logistics: All you need to set up this Kick-Starter is two dozen Ping-Pong balls and a permanent marker. On each ball, write one Between-the-Sheets pair and pile the balls in three or more bowls (to keep guests circulating). If you like, you can put a little sign by each bowl that reads "Between the Sheets . . . Who would you choose?" to give people the idea, but we've found that guests catch on pretty quickly—and figuring out the game is part of the fun.

   To create your Between-the-Sheets choices, use political figures, celebrities, television characters—the options are endless. Tap your crowd's interests: If you know lots of lawyers, make them choose between two Supreme Court justices. If you're from a small town, make them choose between the mayor and the football coach. Don't be limited by whether the people you pick are dead, alive, or even human: We've featured the Terminator, Marilyn Monroe, and even SpongeBob SquarePants. If you stall out at 15 or 20 pairings, don't sweat it. If your friends are anything like ours, once the game starts they'll begin coming up with their own hilarious hypotheticals.

TRADITIONALLY, *this sexy cocktail is served in a martini glass. At our parties, we pour them over ice in short glasses because that's what we have enough of.*

BETWEEN THE SHEETS

TO MAKE ONE DRINK:

> 1 ounce brandy or cognac
> 1 ounce triple sec
> 1 ounce rum
> 1 ounce fresh lemon juice

SHAKE all the ingredients with ice and strain into an ice-filled glass.

TO MAKE A PITCHER (ABOUT 20 DRINKS):

> 2½ cups brandy or cognac
> 2½ cups triple sec
> 2½ cups rum
> 2½ cups fresh lemon juice

COMBINE all the ingredients in a large pitcher, add ice, and stir for 30 seconds. Spoon out the ice cubes. Store the pitcher in the refrigerator until party time.

THE MENU

Foods reputed to have an aphrodisiacal effect—and guaranteed to seduce the taste buds

Olive Crostini with White Truffle Oil

Steak Tartare

Asparagus Parmesan Bites

Artichoke Hearts with Cucumber Aïoli

Green M&M's

indispensable party help: the 6:30 friend

No matter how meticulously you plan, you may find yourself running out of time the day of the party. We've been there. Half an hour before the guests are due to arrive, we'll be congratulating our-selves that the food is ready, when we realize that we haven't lit the candles or washed the last six wine glasses or (and this is when it really gets hairy) figured out what shoes to wear. To the rescue: our 6:30 friend. We highly recommend that you get one of these. Ours is Lauren's old friend Wendy, who by now automatically shows up exactly a half hour before party time and does anything we haven't gotten around to doing. "Wend,

can you squeeze some lime juice?" we'll yell from the bathroom, where we're applying mascara. And Wendy does. She's saved our butts countless times. Keep in mind that someone already living with you—your husband or roommate or sister—cannot be your 6:30 friend. No matter how good your intentions, you will likely have pressed him or her into service long before 6:30. What you're after is someone whose arrival is the signal to start putting the finishing touches on everything. A 6:30 friend comes over already dressed and ready to do what-ever it takes to keep you from wigging out just as you should be settling into gracious hostess mode.

Recipes

olive crostini with white truffle oil

MAKES ABOUT 30 CROSTINI

White truffle oil is what makes these crostini intoxicating. Both the ancient Greeks and the ancient Romans attributed aphrodisiacal powers to the truffle. Your modern-day guests will be able to vouch for its ability to stimulate appetites.

$\frac{1}{2}$ cup finely chopped black olives

$\frac{1}{2}$ cup finely chopped pimiento-stuffed green olives

$\frac{1}{2}$ cup grated Parmesan cheese

2 garlic cloves, minced

2 tablespoons white truffle oil

$\frac{3}{4}$ cup grated Monterey Jack cheese

$\frac{1}{4}$ cup minced parsley

1 skinny baguette

PREHEAT broiler.

COMBINE the black olives, green olives, Parmesan cheese, garlic, and truffle oil in a large bowl and stir until well mixed. Gently stir in the Monterey Jack cheese and parsley.

CUT THE BAGUETTE INTO THIN SLICES. Spread some olive mixture on each slice and broil until the bread is toasted at the edges and the cheese is melted, 3 to 4 minutes.

make-ahead factor: *The olive mixture can be made up to 3 days ahead if you can prevent yourself from sampling it straight out of the bowl. The crostini are just as flavorful at room temperature as warm, so you can broil them several hours before the party.*

steak tartare

Try this once and you'll be addicted. The key to this delicacy is to buy the sirloin from a very good butcher no earlier than the day before you want to use it, so it's at its absolute freshest.

1 pound sirloin steak, trimmed of excess fat

1½ tablespoons minced parsley, plus sprigs for garnish

1½ tablespoons minced red onion

3 teaspoons minced capers, plus whole capers for garnish

1 egg yolk

1½ teaspoons fresh lemon juice

1½ teaspoons extra-virgin olive oil

1 teaspoon Worcestershire sauce

½ teaspoon anchovy paste*

salt and pepper

1 skinny baguette, thinly sliced and toasted

CUT THE BEEF into chunks and pulse in a food processor until just ground. Transfer to a large bowl. Add all the ingredients through the anchovy paste, stirring as gently as possible to avoid turning the meat into mush. Add salt and pepper to taste. Cover tightly with plastic pressed directly against the surface of the steak tartare and chill in the refrigerator for at least 1 hour.

JUST BEFORE THE PARTY, mound the steak tartare in a chilled bowl and garnish with the sprigs of parsley and whole capers. Serve with thin slices of toasted baguette.

ONE IMPORTANT NOTE: Our mom raises beef cattle, so we grew up eating beef in all its forms, including raw. There is, however, the slight risk of contamination by bacteria, so we'd be remiss if we didn't tell you that the USDA advises against the consumption of raw beef and raw eggs by pregnant women, young children, and anyone with a weakened immune system—as well as, we'd add, anyone who's just being cautious.

make-ahead factor: *The tartare can be mixed 4 hours ahead (no more than that) and kept covered and refrigerated.*

---

* *Don't be tempted to leave this out, even if you believe "anchovy" is synonymous with "ruined pizza." You use a small amount, but it makes a big taste difference.*

asparagus parmesan bites

MAKES 80 ASPARAGUS BITES

Working with puff pastry may sound complicated, but you'll be surprised by how easy this recipe is. Don't worry if your hors d'oeuvres look a little lumpy or lopsided when you roll them. In the oven, the pastry turns an appealing golden brown and puffs up, which hides any imperfections.

28 asparagus spears (about 1½ pounds)*

1 (17-ounce) package frozen puff pastry sheets, thawed according to package directions

2 large egg yolks, lightly beaten with 2 tablespoons cold water to make an egg wash

3 cups grated Parmesan cheese

coarse salt

vegetable oil for oiling the baking sheet

PREHEAT oven to 400°F.

SNAP OFF the tough ends of the asparagus spears and blanch them: Drop them into a pot of generously salted, boiling water and cook until you can pierce them with a fork but they're still crisp, 3 to 5 minutes depending on the thickness of the spears. Immediately plunge them into a bowl of ice water until no longer warm. Pat dry with paper towels and set aside.

UNFOLD the pastry sheets and cut each one in half lengthwise. Using a floured rolling pin on a floured surface, roll out one half-sheet into a 7 x 20-inch rectangle (keep the remaining sheets chilled, covered with plastic wrap). Don't worry about being too precise—you can trim the edges with a knife to even them up. Cut the rectangle crosswise into six smaller rectangles (each about 7 x 3 inches).

BRUSH each rectangle with the egg wash and sprinkle evenly with 2 tablespoons of the Parmesan cheese, leaving a half-inch border on the long sides. Lay an asparagus spear along one long side, then roll up the pastry, pressing at the seam to seal. Repeat with all the remaining puff pastry sheets.

* *To get the perfect asparagus-to-pastry ratio, use medium asparagus spears, not the pencil-thin ones or those sequoia-size monsters.*

BRUSH any remaining egg wash on the tops and sides of the rolls. Sprinkle the outsides of the rolls with coarse salt, then arrange them seam side down on a lightly oiled baking sheet. Chill in the refrigerator for about 20 minutes to firm up the pastry.

BAKE until puffed and golden brown, 13 to 15 minutes. Transfer to a cutting board and cut each roll crosswise into three bite-size sections. Serve warm.

make-ahead factor: *The rolls can be baked 4 or 5 hours ahead and kept uncovered at room temperature. Warm them in a 300°F oven for 5 to 7 minutes, then cut them.*

artichoke hearts with cucumber aïoli

MAKES ABOUT 50 PIECES AND ABOUT 1 CUP OF AÏOLI

In sixteenth-century France, only men were allowed to eat artichokes because they were thought to be such a potent aphrodisiac. Thank goodness artichokes are equal-opportunity these days. Aïoli is a traditional garlic mayonnaise that blows store-bought mayo out of the water. When making it, be sure your ingredients and your cooking tools are at room temperature before beginning.

FOR THE AÏOLI

4 garlic cloves, finely minced to the consistency of a paste

2 egg yolks

1 tablespoon Dijon mustard

⅛ teaspoon salt

2 tablespoons fresh lemon juice, plus more to taste

2 cups extra-virgin olive oil

1 medium cucumber

2 tablespoons roughly chopped parsley

FOR THE ARTICHOKE HEARTS

3 (9-ounce) boxes frozen artichoke hearts

2 garlic cloves, crushed

PREPARE THE AÏOLI: Combine the garlic, egg yolks, mustard, salt, and 2 tablespoons lemon juice in a food processor or blender. Process for 30 seconds. With the machine running, gradually add the olive oil through the feed tube, a few drops at a time to start. Continue to slowly add the oil in a fine stream until it has been incorporated and the aïoli is thoroughly blended and has thickened. It will be slightly thinner than commercial mayonnaise. If the aïoli separates, don't panic—it's easily salvageable: Put a single egg yolk in a separate bowl, allow it to come to room temperature, and then whisk the separated aïoli into it, a little at a time, to re-emulsify the sauce. Adjust salt and lemon juice to taste.

PEEL THE CUCUMBER, seed it, and cut it into cubes. Pulse the cukes in the food processor or blender. Pour the pureed cuke into a fine-meshed sieve and press on it with your fingers or the back of a spoon to thoroughly drain the liquid. Gently fold ¼ cup of the cucumber puree and the chopped parsley into the aïoli. Cover and refrigerate for 2 hours before serving to allow the flavors to meld.

PREPARE THE ARTICHOKE HEARTS: Blanch the hearts by dropping them into a pot of generously salted, boiling water with the crushed garlic cloves. Cook for about 4 minutes. Immediately plunge them into a bowl of ice water until they're no longer warm. Pat dry with paper towels. If necessary, cut into bite-size pieces.

SERVE the aïoli in a bowl next to the artichoke hearts with toothpicks on the side.

make-ahead factor: *The artichoke hearts can be prepared up to 2 days ahead and kept covered and refrigerated. The aïoli can be made up to 3 days ahead and kept covered and refrigerated.*

green m&m's

Green M&Ms' aphrodisiacal properties are urban legend, and bowls of them always get a big laugh at this party. Instead of sorting through dozens of bags of mixed M&M's, go to www.mms.com, click on "Colorworks," and order the greenies in bulk, then place them in several bowls.

CARTOONS AND COCKTAILS

We're all fans of weekends, but remember how extra-special Saturday felt when you were a kid? Every other day of the week, waking up early was a drag, but on Saturday, you leapt out of bed at the crack of dawn to watch cartoons. Schoolhouse Rock, Hong Kong Phooey, Scooby-Doo—the characters and songs are probably burned into your brain, especially if you grew up in the '70s or early '80s. This party creates an instant camaraderie among your Saturday-night guests by tapping into that shared nostalgia for Saturday mornings. Don't be surprised if you find you're not the only one who dreamed of headlining with Josie and the Pussycats.

CONVERSATION
KICK-STARTER

The gist: The concept here is super-simple but surprisingly compelling: Throughout the party, stacks of coasters with funny cartoon trivia quizzes and fill-in-the-blank questions take guests back to their Lucky Charms and Looney Tunes days. It's amazing how easily people mix when you give them license to be a little silly. The first time we threw this party, we knew the guests were getting swept up in the fun when we heard a chorus of "Lolly, Lolly, Lolly, get your adverbs here."

The logistics: You'll need 15 to 20 thick paper coasters, which you can buy at paper supply stores and some craft stores. (Or simply use high-quality cocktail napkins.) Write the trivia tidbits on each coaster with a bold marker. To get you started, we've given you some examples from one of our parties, but an Internet search will remind you of cartoon characters you loved, breakfast cereals you begged Mom to buy, and other silly Saturday morning stuff. Plus, you'll probably find, as we did, that some of your guests have a positively unhealthy amount of brain space devoted to cartoon knowledge, and they'll keep the questions and memories rolling!

TO GET YOU STARTED: A SATURDAY-MORNING QUIZ COLLECTION

The answers are at the bottom of the page. If you can answer all the questions without looking, then this party is made for you!

1. Give the next line: "Meet George Jetson. _____"

2. What company makes Wile E. Coyote's always unreliable Roadrunner-catching products?

3. Confess: What's the guilty-pleasure breakfast cereal you've loved since childhood?

4. What's the name of the Scooby-Doo van?

5. Name four cartoon mice.

6. Where does Hong Kong Phooey turn into a superhero?

7. "Conjunction Junction, what's your function?" What's the next line?

8. When the Wonder Twins activate their power, what forms do they take?

9. Name the original shapes and colors of the Lucky Charms marshmallows.

10. Where does Fred Flintstone work?

10. *The Bedrock Gravel Company*

added in 1975.)

9. *Green clovers, yellow moons, pink hearts, orange stars. (Blue diamonds were*

8. *One takes the form of an animal, one takes a water-based form.*

7. *"Hooking up words and phrases and clauses"*

6. *A filing cabinet drawer*

Gonzalez, Mighty Mouse, Danger Mouse

5. *Possible answers: Mickey Mouse, Minnie Mouse, Jerry (of Tom and Jerry), Speedy*

4. *The Mystery Machine*

ren's is Lucky Charms.

3. *The possibilities are endless. Just for the record, Ann's answer is Froot Loops. Lau-*

2. *Acme*

1. *"His boy, Elroy. Daughter Judy, Jane, his wife."*

THE PINK PANTHER'S *pleasingly pink color isn't the only thing that gives it its name. Like a panther, these can sneak up on you!*

PINK PANTHER

TO MAKE ONE DRINK:

> ³/₄ **ounce fresh lime juice**
> ¹/₂ **ounce Rose's Sweetened Lime Juice**
> 1¹/₂ **teaspoons superfine sugar**
> 1¹/₂ **ounces bourbon**
> ¹/₂ **teaspoon grenadine**
> **club soda**

COMBINE the fresh lime juice and Rose's Lime Juice in a glass and stir in the superfine sugar until dissolved. Fill the glass with ice. Add the bourbon and grenadine. Top off with club soda and stir.

TO MAKE A PITCHER (ABOUT 20 DRINKS):

> 1³/₄ **cups plus 2 tablespoons fresh lime juice**
> 1¹/₄ **cups Rose's Sweetened Lime Juice**
> ¹/₂ **cup plus 2 tablespoons superfine sugar**
> 3³/₄ **cups bourbon**
> 3 **tablespoons plus 1 teaspoon grenadine**
> 1¹/₂ **liters club soda**

COMBINE the fresh lime juice and Rose's Lime Juice in a large pitcher. Add the superfine sugar and stir until dissolved. Add the bourbon and grenadine, stir well, and chill until party time. To serve, fill glass with ice and pour each Pink Panther so the glass is half full. Top off with club soda and stir.

Breakfast-inspired but evening-appropriate bites

Spicy Sausage Squares

Caramelized Onion Jam on Toast with Brie

Bacon Blue Cheese Dip

Melon and Prosciutto Skewers

Supercharged Chex Mix

SISTERS' SECRETS TO CONFIDENT HOSTESSING

How to keep warm foods warm

One of the toughest challenges for a host once the party is under way is to keep the hors d'oeuvres that are supposed to be served warm from growing cold and unappetizing on the serving tray. There's no one perfect solution, but over a dozen years of party-throwing, we've come up with a few keep 'em hot hints:

1 **equip yourself:** Our favorite temperature-maintenance method is an electric hot plate or warming tray. Plug it in, put your serving dish on top, and you're assured that warm foods stay that way. We recommend that you find one with a controllable temperature knob rather than just an on-off switch. (Some even include a "hot spot" to keep sauces extra-hot.)

2 **preheat your platters:** Sliding your straight-out-of-the-oven goodies onto a cold serving tray starts the cool-down process before the first guest has a chance to pounce. Instead, warm the platters.

You can run them under hot water or warm them in a 200°F oven, but since we've generally got the sink and oven otherwise employed, we've found a different way: We place all the platters we think we might use in the dishwasher and run a cycle that includes heated drying. We keep the dishwasher door closed until the last minute, then pull out the steaming hot (and, as a bonus, dust-and streak-free) trays.

3 **use the food equivalent of a hot-water bottle:** Fill a cloth bag big enough to cover the bottom of your serving basket or dish with uncooked rice, so it's a couple of inches thick. (We've successfully used the drawstring travel bags that come with some shoes and a clean cotton sock tied off at the top.) Heat the filled bag in the microwave for 2 to 3 minutes until it's hot to the touch. Lay it in the bottom of the dish, cover it with a pretty cloth napkin, and place the food on top.

Recipes

spicy sausage squares

We created this recipe in honor of our mom, who believes just about any dish made with sausage is worth eating.

FOR THE CRUST

1/2 cup (1 stick) butter, softened

3 ounces cream cheese, softened

1/8 teaspoon salt

1 cup all-purpose flour

FOR THE TOPPING

1/2 pound ground pork sausage

1 cup shredded sharp white Cheddar cheese

1 (4–5-ounce) can chopped green chiles, drained

1 tablespoon chopped fresh chives

2 eggs

1 cup milk

1/4 teaspoon salt

dash cayenne pepper

PREPARE THE CRUST: With an electric mixer, beat the butter, cream cheese, and salt until creamy. Blend in the flour, then cover with plastic wrap and refrigerate for 1 hour.

PREHEAT oven to 375°F.

PRESS the chilled dough into a 15 x 10 x 2-inch glass pan to form an even layer covering the bottom. Set aside.

PREPARE THE TOPPING: Crumble the sausage into a small skillet, breaking up any large chunks. Cook over medium heat, stirring frequently, until browned, 8 to 10 minutes. With a slotted spoon, remove the sausage from the skillet and sprinkle it evenly over the dough. Top with the cheese, chiles, and chives. Whisk together the eggs, milk, salt, and cayenne, then pour the mixture over the dough. Bake until the egg mixture is firm in the middle, 35 to 40 minutes.

REMOVE the pan from the oven and let it cool for 10 to 15 minutes. Cut into 1 1/2-inch squares. Serve warm.

make-ahead factor: *The sausage squares can be made up to 2 days ahead and kept covered and refrigerated. Before the party, warm them in a 300°F oven for 6 to 8 minutes.*

caramelized onion jam on toast with brie

MAKES ABOUT 30 PIECES OF TOAST AND 1 CUP OF JAM

Besides being smashing as an hors d'oeuvre, this savory spread will elevate an ordinary sandwich and is great served over chicken and pork chops. Only thing is, you're unlikely to have any left over.

FOR THE JAM

1/4 cup olive oil

2 1/2 cups diced sweet onions, such as Vidalia (about 1 pound)*

3 garlic cloves, minced

1/2 cup chicken stock

1/4 cup balsamic vinegar

2 teaspoons (packed) light brown sugar

1/2 teaspoon dried rosemary, crumbled

2 tablespoons tomato paste

1/4 teaspoon Worcestershire sauce

salt and pepper

FOR THE TOAST

1/2 cup olive oil

1 large garlic clove, crushed

15 slices cocktail-size white or rye bread

1 wedge Brie, 10 to 12 ounces

PREPARE THE JAM: Heat the olive oil in a large skillet over medium heat. Add the onions and garlic and sauté, stirring frequently, until the onions just begin to brown, 10 to 12 minutes. Add the chicken stock and simmer until most of the liquid has evaporated, about 5 minutes. Add the balsamic vinegar, brown sugar, and rosemary and cook another 5 minutes. Stir in the tomato paste and Worcestershire sauce, then reduce the heat to low and simmer until the jam thickens, 2 to 3 more minutes. Add salt and pepper to taste.

PREHEAT oven to 375°F.

PREPARE THE TOAST: In a microwave oven, heat the olive oil and crushed garlic clove for 15 to 20 seconds to infuse the oil with garlic. Discard the garlic. Brush one side of each slice of bread with the oil, then halve diagonally. Bake until crisp and lightly browned, 10 to 12 minutes.

TO SERVE, bring the wedge of Brie to room temperature. Serve it alongside the onion jam (which can be served warm or at room temperature) and toast.

make-ahead factor: *The jam can be made 3 to 6 days ahead and kept covered and refrigerated. Bring it to room temperature before serving. The toast can be made several hours ahead. Allow it to cool, then wrap tightly in aluminum foil.*

* *We grew up eating Vidalia sweet onions, but any variety will do. You might find Maui or Walla Walla onions, or your supermarket may just label them, as ours does, "sweet onions."*

bacon blue cheese dip

MAKES ABOUT 2 CUPS OF DIP

Although we generally think of celery sticks as the least glamorous of crudités, with this dip celery just seems right. That nice, clean crunch is the perfect partner for the assertiveness of blue cheese.

1/2 cup sour cream	1 garlic clove, minced
3 ounces cream cheese	1/2 teaspoon lemon juice
10 slices bacon, plus 1 slice for garnish, cooked until crisp	1/4 teaspoon Tabasco sauce
	1/4 teaspoon celery seeds
5 tablespoons crumbled blue cheese	celery sticks for dipping

COMBINE the ingredients through the celery seeds in a food processor and blend until smooth. Transfer to a serving bowl and chill in the refrigerator until party time. Garnish with crumbled bacon. Serve with celery sticks, sliced on the diagonal and with any tough strings removed.

make-ahead factor: *The dip can be made 3 to 4 days ahead and kept covered and refrigerated. Keep in mind that the blue-cheese flavor intensifies with time.*

melon and prosciutto skewers

MAKES 32 SKEWERS

Melon and prosciutto are a classic combination. We added a flavor kick and created easy-to-eat "kebabs" to turn it into cocktail party–appropriate finger food.

4 tablespoons balsamic vinegar

4 tablespoons chopped fresh basil

2 tablespoons sugar

1 ripe honeydew melon, peeled, seeded, and cut into 32 bite-size chunks*

¾ pound thin prosciutto slices

IN A SMALL BOWL, stir together the vinegar, basil, and sugar until the sugar dissolves. Let the mixture stand for 30 minutes, then pour it through a fine-meshed strainer set over a large bowl, pressing against the chopped basil to extract all the flavor. Put the melon chunks in the strained vinegar mixture, toss to coat, and let stand for 30 minutes.

MAKE SURE you have 32 slices of prosciutto, cutting slices in half lengthwise if necessary. Fold each slice up accordion-style and thread onto a skewer or toothpick. Follow it with a melon chunk so the hors d'oeuvres can be arranged standing up on a platter, each skewer sticking out the top.

make-ahead factor: *The vinegar mixture can be made 2 days ahead and kept covered and refrigerated. The melon chunks can be cut (but not marinated) 1 day ahead and kept covered and refrigerated.*

* *We sometimes see supermarket shoppers pressing on honeydew melons in order to find one that's ripe. Unfortunately, that won't tell you much. Instead, run your fingertips over the melon. If the rind is slightly tacky to the touch (it feels like rubbing your finger along a rubber band), the melon is ripe; if your fingers skate smoothly over the rind, keep looking—or allow a few days for the melon to ripen on your counter.*

supercharged chex mix

MAKES 12 CUPS OF MIX

We've revved up the classic recipe from the back of the Chex box for this bowl food. Feel free to take it even further: Throw in mixed nuts, popcorn, broken bread sticks, or whatever strikes your fancy.

6 cups mixed Chex cereal (rice, corn, wheat)

1½ cups thin pretzels

1½ cups rice crackers, broken into bite-size pieces if bigger than bite-size

1½ cups bagel chips, broken into pieces if bigger than bite-size

1½ cups corn chips, such as Fritos

4 tablespoons (½ stick) butter

1 garlic clove, crushed

1 tablespoon Worcestershire sauce

1 teaspoon ground cumin

½ teaspoon chili powder

¼ teaspoon cayenne

¼ teaspoon salt or onion salt

PREHEAT oven to 250°F.

TOSS the first five ingredients together in a large bowl. In a small saucepan, melt the butter over moderate heat with the crushed garlic clove, then stir in the Worcestershire sauce and spices. Continue to heat until hot but not boiling. (This can also be done in a microwave oven.) Remove the garlic clove.

DRIZZLE the butter mixture over the dry ingredients and toss until completely coated. Spread the mix in a shallow layer in a large roasting pan or baking sheet. Bake 1 hour, then allow to cool completely.

make-ahead factor: *The mix can be made 1 week ahead and kept at room temperature in an airtight container.*

HE SAID, SHE SAID
A soirée where the sexes square off

Men never ask for directions. Women take forever to get ready. Men leave the toilet seat up. Women go to the restroom in packs. We all know the clichés, and we all have an opinion about them—and usually a funny story by way of illustration. Nothing kicks off heated and hilarious discussion—even among strangers—like an organized battle of the sexes.

Conversation
Kick-Starter

The gist: This party pits the men against the women, prompting good-natured argument and plenty of interaction. At the bar, as guests arm themselves for battle with a signature cocktail (pink for women, blue for men), they also load up on marbles (you guessed it: pink marbles for women, blue marbles for men). As they mingle and move around the party, party-goers place their marbles in glasses or jars to cast their votes on a series of He Said/She Said statements, some provocative, some just plain funny. For instance: "Sex on the first date: Great start or Doomed relationship?" "Breasts: Bigger is not always better or Who're you kidding? Yes it is!" The colored marbles pile up in the clear containers, making the gender divide (believe us, there always is one) easy to see. Along the way, the marble voting is often forgotten as your guests stand and debate the topics right then and there.

The logistics: The number of He Said/She Said "voting stations" you set up is entirely flexible, but we usually have five or six—enough so the voting gains momentum but not so many that it feels like an endurance test. Create a card for each station—in addition to the ideas above, we've given you more inspiration in "To get you started: More He Said/She Said topics." Use your imagination to play off recent news events, movies, and the like, and remember that relationships are an inexhaustible source of hot-button topics. On each card, write one answer choice near the left edge, the other near the right and stand the card between two glasses into which guests will drop their marbles to "vote" (think of these as the "ballot boxes").

Place two bowls of colored marbles (available at crafts stores or housewares stores like Pottery Barn) near the bar, the pink ones labeled "For the women," the blue ones labeled "For the men." We recommend providing a multitude of marbles—at one of our He Said/She Said parties, a couple of determined (and perhaps slightly intoxicated) men began stuffing the ballot box with blue marbles on the question of whether the man should pay for dinner on the first date. When a few of the women discovered what was going on, a fierce but friendly voting war began.

TO GET YOU STARTED: MORE HE SAID/SHE SAID TOPICS

- *Manicures for men:* vain and a little prissy *or* just good grooming?

- *Who should pay the first-date dinner tab?* The man—classic dating codes still apply *or* They should split it—it's not the 1950s anymore.

- *Glass ceiling:* relic *or* reality?

- *Fantasy football:* sign of arrested development *or* legitimate leisure activity?

- *Women smoking cigars:* sorta sexy *or* kinda gross?

- *"I'll call you":* truth *or* fiction?

- *Sandals on men:* perfectly acceptable *or* only if you're Jesus?

- *A woman president in the next 5 years:* without a doubt *or* don't count on it?

IN HOMAGE TO *one of classic TV's most argumentative couples, serve Archies and Ediths. Though the blue-tinged Archies are meant for the men and the pink Ediths are for the ladies, we always encourage cross-drinking.*

ARCHIE

TO MAKE ONE DRINK:

> 1 ounce gin
> 1/2 ounce Cointreau
> 1/2 ounce Rose's Sweetened Lime Juice
> 1/2 ounce blue curaçao

SHAKE all the ingredients with ice and strain into an ice-filled glass.

TO MAKE A PITCHER (ABOUT 20 DRINKS):

> 2 1/2 cups gin
> 1 1/4 cups Cointreau
> 1 1/4 cups Rose's Sweetened Lime Juice
> 1 1/4 cups blue curaçao

POUR all the ingredients in a large pitcher, add ice, and stir for about 30 seconds. Spoon out the ice cubes. Store the pitcher in the refrigerator until party time.

* *To make simple syrup: Place equal amounts sugar and water in a small saucepan over medium heat. Stir until the sugar is dissolved and the mixture comes to a boil. Remove from heat and let cool. Store in the refrigerator.*
** *You can use the juice that comes with the cherries, but it's more economical to buy the juice without the cherries if your supermarket carries it.*

EDITH

TO MAKE ONE DRINK:

> 3/4 ounce Calvados
> 1/4 ounce fresh lemon juice
> 1/4 ounce fresh lime juice
> 3/4 teaspoon maraschino cherry juice (spooned off the top of the jar of cherries)
> 1/4 teaspoon simple syrup*
> 1 ounce chilled sparkling apple cider

SHAKE all the ingredients except the sparkling cider with ice and strain into an ice-filled glass. Add the cider and stir.

TO MAKE A PITCHER (ABOUT 20 DRINKS):

> 1 3/4 cups plus 2 tablespoons Calvados
> 1/2 cup plus 2 tablespoons fresh lemon juice
> 1/2 cup plus 2 tablespoons fresh lime juice
> generous 1/4 cup maraschino cherry juice**
> 3 scant tablespoons simple syrup
> 20 ounces chilled sparkling apple cider (about 1 bottle)

COMBINE all the ingredients except the sparkling cider in a large pitcher, add ice, and stir for about 30 seconds. Spoon out the ice cubes. Store the pitcher in the refrigerator until party time. To serve, pour each drink over ice, then add about 1 ounce of cider.

THE MENU

Foods that can be easily picked up, allowing guests to eat as they make the rounds

Bite-Size Crab Cakes with Lemon Caper Mayo

Chicken and Red Onion in Phyllo Cups

Top-Your-Own New Potatoes

Fresh Tomato Bruschetta

Wasabi-Crusted Peas

SISTERS' SECRETS TO CONFIDENT HOSTESSING
what to do if you run out of hors d'oeuvres

No hostess wants to run short on food, but try to keep it in perspective: It's actually a compliment to your cooking. Wouldn't it be a lot worse to have the guests leave most of the food on the table? If you follow our how-many-to-make hors d'oeuvre guidelines on page 7, you should have plenty of food to last the evening, but there are always occasions when you look up and discover that a swarm of locusts has descended while you were nursing your cocktail. When that happens, all you need is a moderate level of aplomb and a back-up dessert item—something low-key and no-assembly-required, such as a few bunches of grapes and some chocolates or after-dinner mints.

The trick is to act as though this is all part of your master plan. Immediately remove all the serving trays from the room, including those that have a few straggler items remaining, as if to signal that you're deliberately ending the hors d'oeuvres portion of the evening. Then put out the platter with your dessert items. Keep the bar open, so guests don't interpret this as a signal that they should leave (unless, of course, that's what you're hoping for).

Recipes

bite-size crab cakes with lemon caper mayo

MAKES ABOUT 40 CRAB CAKES AND 1½ CUPS OF MAYO

There's much debate about how to make the perfect crab cake. Some people will tell you that using saltine crackers or bread crumbs is heresy, but we find the saltines help the cakes hold their shape yet still let the crab flavor come through. This is one of those deceptively easy hors d'oeuvres that guests think you slaved over.

FOR THE MAYO

1 cup mayonnaise

4 tablespoons chopped chives

3 tablespoons lemon juice

1 tablespoon drained capers, roughly chopped

1 teaspoon grated lemon peel

½ teaspoon liquid from the caper jar

FOR THE CRAB CAKES

½ cup mayonnaise

2 eggs, lightly beaten

1 garlic clove, minced

1 tablespoon Dijon mustard

2 teaspoons Worcestershire sauce

pinch salt

1 pound lump crabmeat, drained and picked over to remove any shell*

1 cup finely crushed saltine crackers (from 25 to 28 crackers)**

vegetable oil for oiling the baking sheet

PREPARE THE MAYO: Mix all the ingredients in a small bowl.

PREHEAT broiler.

PREPARE THE CRAB CAKES: In a large bowl, mix the first six ingredients until thoroughly blended. Gently stir in the crabmeat and saltines. Form the mixture into 1-inch balls and arrange them on a lightly oiled baking sheet. Gently press each ball until it flattens into a cake about 1½ to 2 inches across. Broil the crab cakes, turning once halfway through, until they're browned on both sides, 5 to 6 minutes. Serve warm.

make-ahead factor: *The crab cakes can be made 1 day ahead and kept covered and refrigerated. Warm them in a 300°F oven for 5 to 7 minutes. The lemon caper mayo can be made 3 to 4 days ahead and kept covered and refrigerated.*

* *Use fresh or, if fresh isn't available, frozen, but not canned.*
** *You can use a food processor to do this, but we hate to haul ours out for just one quick task. Our easy low-tech method: Put the saltines in a resealable plastic bag, squeeze out the extra air, and seal. Use a rolling pin to crush them inside the bag until finely ground.*

chicken and red onion in phyllo cups

MAKES ABOUT 40 PHYLLO CUPS

Attention, phyllo-phobics! Don't be daunted by this recipe. Phyllo dough is a lot more forgiving than you might think. When serving these, you may want to provide small plates for your guests—they're a little crumbly (but oh so melt-in-your-mouthy).

FOR THE PHYLLO CUPS

1 package phyllo pastry sheets (17 x 12-inch sheets), thawed according to package directions

4 tablespoons (½ stick) unsalted butter, melted, plus more for buttering the muffin tin

FOR THE FILLING

3 to 6 cups chicken broth

3 to 4 skinless boneless chicken breast halves (about 1 pound total)

1 tablespoon olive oil

¾ cup diced red onion

3 tablespoons dry white wine or sherry

2 teaspoons finely chopped fresh thyme

½ cup crumbled feta cheese

PREHEAT oven to 350°F. Generously butter a 12-cup mini-muffin tin.

PREPARE THE CUPS: Cover the stack of phyllo sheets with a clean, damp kitchen towel to keep them from drying out. Put one phyllo sheet on a work surface and brush with melted butter. Cut the sheet in half lengthwise, then cut each half in half again lengthwise, which will result in four strips, each 3 inches wide. Place the four strips, each butter side up, on top of one another. Use a 3-inch round cookie cutter to cut out five rounds (each made up of four layers) or simply cut across the stacks to form 3-inch squares (you'll have a little dough left over).

PRESS each stack of dough into a muffin cup so that the dough comes just to the top of the cup (trim the edges with kitchen shears or a knife if necessary). Bake until golden and crisp, 6 to 8 minutes. Remove to a rack to cool. Repeat until you've used all the phyllo.

REDUCE oven to 300°F.

PREPARE THE FILLING: In a large skillet, put enough broth (about 2 inches) to cover a single layer of chicken breast halves. Bring the liquid to a boil. Add the chicken breasts. Reduce to a simmer and poach the chicken, turning once halfway through, until no longer pink in the middle, 8 to 10 minutes. Remove the chicken from the skillet and finely chop.

DISCARD the chicken cooking liquid and in the same skillet, heat the olive oil. Add the diced onion and cook over moderate heat, stirring, until very tender (some pieces will be browned at the edges), about 3 minutes. Add the wine or sherry and chopped thyme and cook until the liquid has evaporated, another minute or so. Remove the skillet from the heat and stir in the chopped chicken and feta cheese.

SPOON a tablespoon of the filling into each phyllo cup. Bake the filled cups for 3 to 4 minutes until warmed.

make-ahead factor: *The phyllo cups can be baked 3 days ahead, cooled completely, and stored tightly covered at room temperature. They can be frozen for a month. The filling can be made 1 day ahead and kept covered and refrigerated. Bring it to room temperature before filling the cups. Warm the filled cups in a 300°F oven for 6 to 8 minutes.*

top-your-own new potatoes

MAKES 2 TO 3 POTATOES PER GUEST

Guests love hors d'oeuvres that they can "customize" to their own taste. (The mini pork tenderloin sandwiches on page 92 are another example.) Serve these tender little potatoes with one, two, or all of the suggested toppings, depending on how much time you have.

2 to 3 small new potatoes per guest (about 3 pounds for 20 guests)*

PLACE THE POTATOES in a deep stockpot and add water to just cover them. Generously salt the water and bring it to a boil over high heat. Reduce to a simmer and cook until potatoes are easily pierced with a fork, 10 to 15 minutes. Drain and let cool.

WHEN THE POTATOES are cool enough to handle, use a paring knife to cut an X ½ inch to 1 inch deep, depending on how big the potatoes are. The idea is for guests to be able to pinch the potato, squeezing the X open, so they can spoon toppings onto it. Serve the potatoes warm.

NO EFFORT: Serve with a bowl of crème fraîche or sour cream, and a small dish of sea salt.

LOW EFFORT: In addition to crème fraîche and salt, also offer one or two nut oils or flavored olive oils (two of our favorites for these potatoes are walnut oil and basil-flavored olive oil). Let guests know the flavors with small labels.

MO' EFFORT: Make the onion jam on page 59 or a half-recipe of the bacon blue cheese dip on page 60.

make-ahead factor: *The potatoes can be cooked the morning of the party and kept loosely covered at room temperature. Before the party, cut an X in each one, then warm them in a 300°F oven for 7 to 10 minutes.*

---

* *We like red-skinned potatoes, but any variety will do. If you can select them individually, try to pick potatoes that are close to the same size, to make cooking them evenly easier.*

How to cut down on kitchen time— or avoid it altogether

If you've got more money than time, consider buying your hors d'oeuvres ready-made (or partially ready-made). Here are two tricks that have worked for us in a pinch:

1 get thee to the supermarket. At fancier food stores and many bulk food clubs, you can find trays of frozen hors d'oeuvres such as bacon-wrapped scallops and mini spring rolls that can save you hours in the kitchen. And even in standard supermarkets, you can find helpful shortcut products—we're fans of preformed phyllo-dough cups, which save you the step of baking your own (though at twice the price). The secret to making store-bought hors d'oeuvres special is to serve them with your own sauce or dip. Sauces are usually quick to whip up and can be made several days ahead of time, so they won't derail a tight schedule. And when someone compliments your splendid spring rolls with sweet-sour sauce, you can be ready with one of our favorite phrases: "Thanks. It's the sauce that really makes the dish." (By the way, that sauce recipe is on page 109.)

2 order takeout. Restaurants can be a great source for hors d'oeuvres:

- Japanese—Sushi rolls are an obvious choice, but also consider yakitori (grilled chicken skewers) and shrimp shumai (small dumplings, which are easily skewered with a tooth-pick or picked up individually).

- Chinese—Spring rolls (but not egg rolls, which are difficult to cut into individual pieces) and shrimp toasts travel well and taste great.

- Mexican—Everybody loves chips and a made-that-day guacamole, and there are lots of heartier options. Order a selection of quesadillas; ask for them whole, then cut them into bite-size wedges at home. And check the menu for other hors d'oeuvre-size dishes—often, larger Mexican specialties like empanadas show up in the appetizer section as downsized versions (empanaditas).

- Greek—Stuffed grape leaves and spanakopita (phyllo triangles filled with spinach and feta cheese) look gorgeous and can be bought a day or two ahead of time. Plus, you can't go wrong with any Greek dip served with pita bread.

fresh tomato bruschetta

MAKES ABOUT 50 BRUSCHETTA

I f you can, make the tomato topping a day ahead so the flavors have plenty of time to meld. Though you usually see bruschetta served individually, allowing guests to assemble their own saves you tons of time pre-party, plus keeps the bread from getting soggy.

FOR THE TOPPING

8 ripe plum tomatoes, finely diced

2 tablespoons finely minced garlic

1/2 cup coarsely chopped fresh basil

1/4 cup finely chopped fresh parsley

1 1/2 tablespoons extra-virgin olive oil

1 tablespoon fresh lemon juice

1 teaspoon finely minced fresh tarragon or marjoram

1/4 teaspoon crushed red pepper flakes

salt and pepper

FOR THE BRUSCHETTA

2 baguettes

6 garlic cloves

PREPARE THE TOPPING: In a large bowl, combine all the ingredients and mix well. Add salt and pepper to taste. Set aside (unrefrigerated) for at least 3 hours and up to 6 hours.

PREHEAT oven to 350°F.

PREPARE THE BRUSCHETTA: Cut the baguettes into 1/2-inch-thick slices, arrange on a baking sheet, and bake until lightly toasted, 8 to 10 minutes. Meanwhile, cut the garlic cloves in half and, when the bread comes out of the oven, rub the cut side of the garlic on one side of each slice of bread.

SERVE the tomato mixture in a bowl surrounded by the toasts and let guests assemble the bruschetta themselves.

make-ahead factor: *The tomato mixture is best made 6 hours ahead and kept covered but not refrigerated.*

wasabi-crusted peas

We first discovered dried peas coated with wasabi, or Japanese horseradish, in a little take-out sushi joint near our New York apartment. We quickly found ourselves devoted to their crunchy texture and spicy kick and frequently bought three or four bags at a time. If you don't find bags of the peas at your supermarket, look for them where bulk snacks are sold in those big plastic, scoop-it-yourself bins. Place them in bowls around the room. One caution: Make sure to get peas that are clearly labeled "hot." The nonspicy ones aren't nearly as interesting.

A WINE-TASTING PARTY
EVEN BEER DRINKERS WILL LOVE

We've been to those stuffy wine tastings where a snooty sommelier pours you a driplet of wine and expects you to swirl, swish, spit, and say something erudite. They're a little nerve-wracking—and that's not fun. At our version of a wine tasting, your guests don't have to know anything at all about wine, they just have to drink it. We've never encountered any resistance there!

Conversation
KICK-STARTER

The gist: In several spots in your entertaining area, set up tasting stations, each with a pair of related but different wines—a French Merlot and an Argentinian Merlot, for instance—with their labels covered. Provide a card with a brief description of each wine's flavors and aromas. Guests pour themselves samples of both wines and try to match each one to the correct description. Even wine-phobics often prove to be surprisingly good at detecting flavors like cherry and smoke once they're cued to look for them, and as guests move through the party, tasting at their own pace, they comfortably compare notes and discuss what they're drinking.

The logistics: Unless you're a wine connoisseur, enlist a wine merchant to help you with the tasting notes. Tell him or her that you're planning a wine-tasting party and want to buy all the wine at his store (that should put you on friendly terms). With your merchant's help, choose four or five pairs of wines, some red, some white, and ask for written descriptions of each one (most good wine stores have access to tasting notes written by experts). Explain that you want to focus on the taste and smell of the wines, not what kind of soil it was grown in or what foods it goes best with. You'll need approximately one bottle of each wine for every 15 to 20 guests.

Using one card for each pair of wines, write down the name of each wine, followed by the brief description. Using the pair of Merlots as an example, your card would look something like this:

Domaine de St. Antoine Merlot (France)
An intense aroma of fresh blackberries, black pepper, cherries, and plums. Delicate oak and a touch of earth in the flavor.

Santa Julia Merlot (Argentina)
Much more—and much riper—fruit in both the smell and taste: ripe plums and black cherries, blackberry jam, plus a touch of vanilla.

Next, wrap each wine duo in contrasting wine bags—silver for the French Merlot and gold for the Argentinian Merlot, say. (You can get these at your wine store, or wherever you usually buy gift wrap.) Tie the bags closed at the neck to prevent peeking. To help you keep track while you're wrapping all the bottles, it's a good idea to put a sticky note on each bag reminding you which wine is which. Finally, on the back of each description card, create an answer key so guests can find out immediately if they've guessed correctly. For example:

SILVER: DOMAINE DE ST. ANTOINE (FRANCE)

GOLD: SANTA JULIA (ARGENTINA)

Chill the wrapped white wines. Just before party time, uncork the bottles. (If you've purchased more than one bottle of each wine to be tasted, we recommend opening only one at a time. You may be surprised by how far one bottle will go.) Set the bottles up in the proper pairs around your home (scrap the sticky notes). As your guests arrive, briefly explain how the tasting works. Give each person a wine glass and suggest that he or she start with the whites and progress to the reds. (Wine purists would demand a fresh glass for each wine, but then, that's why we don't invite them!)

SIGNATURE COCKTAILS

Wine, wine, and more wine. No, it's not technically cocktails, but your guests won't complain.

THE MENU

In keeping with the very informal idea of wine-tasting here, we've ignored any so-called rules about matching foods with particular wines or colors of wine. All that matters is that everything tastes great.

Tandoori Lamb with Cumin Dipping
Sauce Zesty Baked Zucchini Squares
Crostini with Tapenade
Savory Cheese Puffs
Wine Crackers

Two simple steps to making the room look elegant

We've read entertaining books that devote whole chapters to choosing just the right flowers for table centerpieces, or that describe in elaborate detail how to drape bed sheets from the ceiling to create an exotic atmosphere. Well, forget about all that. Your guests are there to drink your creative cocktails, eat your delicious food, and talk to all the terrific people you've invited, not to admire your prowess with a staple gun. All you need to make your party space feel festive is the right lighting, which is easy to achieve and costs next to nothing.

STEP 1: BEWARE THE GLARE

Take a look at the lamps and overhead lights in your main party space. In Lauren's apartment, where we usually entertain, there's an overhead fixture near the front door, plus four lamps in the living room. With all of them on, the room is so blindingly bright you could perform surgery. Too much wattage makes party guests feel exposed and uncomfortable; to encourage easy mingling and conversation, keep the lighting at a kind of twilight level—think of the atmosphere of a romantic restaurant. Just before a party, we exchange the 100-watt bulb that's usually in the entryway fixture for a pink-tinted 40-watt bulb. As soon as guests enter, the soft, diffuse light signals a mood switch into relaxed party mode. We make the same bulb switch in the table lamps, and we keep the standing lamps, which have dimmers, dialed to a medium-low glow.

STEP 2: INCREASE YOUR CANDLE POWER

Candlelight does more to make a room look beautiful and feel inviting than a truckload of flowers. Use inexpensive votive candles all over your home—not just the main party space, but in any room guests might go into, including the bathrooms. A few things to keep in mind:

- Never use scented candles. They interfere with the fragrance and flavor of the food.

- Don't place candles near potential sitting areas or on surfaces where guests might like to set down their drinks. We've got wide windowsills, which people always tend to perch on, so even though candles look gorgeous in the window, we limit them to higher ledges and out-of-the-way corners.

- Though a votive candle is a tiny little thing, keep in mind that five, 10, or more of them in a moderate-sized room will raise the temperature noticeably. (And when the room is full of guests, the temp will rise by a few degrees more.) Adjust your air conditioner to cool the room before guests arrive or open some windows to compensate.

Recipes

tandoori lamb with cumin dipping sauce

MAKES ABOUT 60 PIECES

One of us (we'll never tell who) is notorious for not reading to the end of a recipe and then finding out in the middle that it requires that something marinate overnight. So consider this a heads-up: The lamb needs to marinate overnight. The cool cumin dipping sauce is the perfect complement to the rich, savory taste of the lamb.

FOR THE LAMB

2 cups plain yogurt

2 tablespoons ground coriander

2 tablespoons paprika

2 tablespoons fresh lemon juice

$1^1/_2$ tablespoons ground cumin

$1^1/_2$ tablespoons ground ginger

$^1/_2$ teaspoon turmeric

$^1/_2$ teaspoon ground cardamom

$^1/_2$ teaspoon salt

1 garlic clove, minced

2 pounds boneless leg of lamb, trimmed of fat and cut into 1-inch cubes

vegetable oil for oiling the pan

FOR THE DIPPING SAUCE

$^3/_4$ cup sour cream

$^3/_4$ cup plain yogurt

1 tablespoon fresh lemon juice

1 teaspoon ground cumin

salt and pepper

MARINATE THE LAMB: Combine everything except the lamb and the oil in a bowl and blend thoroughly. Add the lamb, stirring to fully coat each cube. Cover and refrigerate overnight.

PREPARE THE DIPPING SAUCE: Mix all the ingredients together in a bowl. Add salt and pepper to taste.

PREHEAT broiler.

REMOVE the lamb from the marinade and gently pat off extra marinade with paper towels. Transfer to a lightly oiled broiler pan and broil 3 minutes. Turn the cubes over and broil another 2 minutes. The lamb should be slightly pink in the center. Transfer the lamb to a plate or cutting board and sprinkle with salt.

LOW EFFORT: Arrange the lamb on a platter and provide toothpicks for guests to make their own "instant skewers." Offer the cumin dipping sauce on the side.

MO' EFFORT: Cut naan (Indian flatbread) or another flatbread, such as pita, into small rectangles or wedges and serve with the dipping sauce alongside so guests can create miniature sandwiches.

make-ahead factor: *Both the marinade and the dipping sauce can be made 2 days ahead and kept covered and refrigerated. The lamb is best broiled close to party time and served warm. However, in our small apartment, using the broiler tends to raise the room temperature, so we broil before the party starts and then warm the lamb in a 400°F oven for about 5 minutes. This can be done at the same time you bake the savory cheese puffs.*

zesty baked zucchini squares

MAKES ABOUT 100 SQUARES

The recipe for this simple, savory dish originally came from our mom, who's made it for years. She says it's the one her friends and party guests most often ask her to share.

1 cup Bisquick

1/2 cup finely diced onion

1/2 cup grated Parmesan cheese

1/2 cup vegetable oil

4 eggs, lightly beaten

2 tablespoons chopped fresh parsley

1 1/2 garlic cloves, finely chopped

1/2 teaspoon salt

1/2 teaspoon dried oregano

dash pepper

3 cups thinly sliced unpeeled zucchini (4 to 5 small zucchini)*

butter for buttering the baking dish

PREHEAT oven to 350°F. Combine all the ingredients except the zucchini and butter in a large bowl and mix thoroughly. Add the zucchini and gently stir to separate and coat each slice. Spread the mixture in a lightly buttered 12x 9 x2 pan and bake until it is golden brown and pulls away slightly from the pan at the edges, 20 to 25 minutes. Let cool 10 to 15 minutes, then cut into 1-inch squares.

make-ahead factor: *The dish can be made 2 days ahead and kept covered and refrigerated. Cut into squares and warm them in a 300°F oven for 6 to 8 minutes before serving.*

* *The thinner the zucchini slices, the better; they're easier to bite through. We use the slicing disk on the food processor, but you can do this by hand with a box grater (use the long curved slits on the side).*

crostini with tapenade

MAKES 25 TO 30 CROSTINI AND ABOUT 1 CUP OF TAPENADE

This is one of our "in case of emergency" hors d'oeuvres—it takes about two minutes to make and all the ingredients are things that keep nearly forever in the fridge or kitchen cabinet. (If you don't have a baguette, the tapenade is just as good on crackers.)

FOR THE TAPENADE

1 cup pitted Kalamata olives

4 anchovy fillets

2 tablespoons capers, drained

2 tablespoons extra-virgin olive oil

¼ teaspoon very finely minced garlic

FOR THE CROSTINI

1 skinny loaf of Italian or French bread

extra-virgin olive oil

PREPARE THE TAPENADE: Combine all the ingredients in a food processor and pulse until the tapenade is finely chopped, but not pureed. It should have a slightly rough texture.

PREHEAT oven to 350°F.

PREPARE THE CROSTINI: Thinly slice the bread and drizzle it lightly on one side with the olive oil.

BAKE until lightly toasted, 8 to 10 minutes.

make-ahead factor: *The tapenade can be made up to 1 week ahead and kept covered and refrigerated. The crostini can be toasted 1 day ahead and kept at room temperature in a resealable plastic bag.*

savory cheese puffs

MAKES ABOUT 32 PUFFS

What's not to love about an hors d'oeuvre that looks and tastes sophisticated but is simple to create? We like to keep a stash of these puffs in the freezer in case of unexpected guests. And unexpected cravings.

4 tablespoons (¹/₂ stick) butter	¹/₄ ¹/₈ teaspoon baking powder
¹/₂ cup milk	2 eggs
¹/₂ teaspoon salt	¹/₂ cup grated Gruyère cheese
¹/₂ teaspoon white pepper	coarse salt
¹/₂ cup all-purpose flour, sifted	

move flour

PREHEAT oven to 400°F.

LINE a baking sheet with parchment paper.

COMBINE the butter, milk, salt, and white pepper in a saucepan over medium heat. When the mixture begins to boil, remove it from the heat and add the flour and baking powder. Stir with a wooden spoon until the mixture pulls away from the sides of the pan and forms a ball (this happens almost immediately). Beat in the eggs one at a time, making sure each egg is fully incorporated. Stir in the cheese.

DROP the mixture in rounded teaspoons about 1 inch apart on the baking sheet. Sprinkle each with coarse salt. Bake until golden brown and puffed, 15 to 20 minutes. Serve warm.

make-ahead factor: *The uncooked individual puffs can be made 2 to 3 weeks ahead. Freeze them on a baking sheet until hard, then transfer them to a freezer bag or container. To serve, remove from freezer, transfer directly to a parchment paper-lined baking sheet without thawing and bake at 400°F until golden brown and puffed, 20 to 25 minutes.*

wine crackers

At a truly proper wine tasting, you might be served wine crackers—the bland ones meant to cleanse the delicate palates of connoisseurs between sips. If you'd like to go that route, you can find the crackers at gourmet stores and wine shops. Since we're already playing fast and loose with all those proper trappings, we go a step further and serve crackers that have a little flavor. Oyster crackers are reminiscent of wine crackers yet are nicely salty. Place bowls of them throughout the room.

A MAKE-YOUR-OWN MARTINI PARTY

Nothing starts a conversation like collaboration. Give your guests a handful of martini recipes and the ingredients to mix the drinks themselves, and before too long they'll be urging each other to experiment, trading sips of their cocktail creations, and mingling easily.

CONVERSATION
KICK-STARTER

The gist: You provide printed recipes for three different martini-style drinks, the liquors and mixers that go in them, and an assortment of jiggers for measuring, shakers for mixing, and strainers for pouring (also a good idea: towels for catching spills). Each recipe makes two drinks, so right off the bat guests are encouraged to share. As everyone gets in touch with his or her inner bartender, both the cocktails and the conversation flow. Of course, it doesn't hurt that martinis and their brethren are perhaps the cocktail world's most potent social lubricants.

The logistics: Set up one big table as the martini mixing station. By corralling all the cocktail activity, you minimize the potential for mess and also create a central gathering place in the room. To protect the table, we put a plastic tablecloth or shower curtain liner on top of it, covered with cloth. The protective plastic lining was an addition we made after our first experience throwing this party, when our good friend Doug decided to show off a little, flipping vodka bottles from hand to hand and pouring drinks from four feet above the glasses. Needless to say, he made a huge mess—and was also the hit of the evening. You may not have a Doug at your party, but even the most careful guest is likely to slosh or spill a little. Remember: That's part of the fun. You can throw this party in the backyard or use card tables instead of your fine furniture if you're concerned, but whatever you do, create a space that will put your mind at ease so you can enjoy yourself.

Next, assemble your equipment:

WHAT TO BUY

- The liquors and mixers for each drink, plus any garnishes, such as cherries.

- Plenty of paper cocktail napkins.

- Ice (see "The ins and outs of ice," page 96, for guidance on how much you'll need).

- Enough cocktail shakers (with lids) to bring your supply up to five or six for a party of 20 or so people making three different drinks. Make sure each is accompanied by a strainer.

- Three jiggers or measuring cups that show ounces.

- One martini glass per guest. (Or see "A smart solution for a glassware shortage," below.)

Now you're ready to set up your martini mixing stations: Print out or hand-write the drink recipes. Assemble the ingredients for each drink in little group-ings with the recipe card, one or two shakers, a strainer, at least one jigger, and a bucket or bowl of ice. Make sure you have an easy-to-get-to sink or an empty ice bucket so people can dump melted ice out of their shakers (or martinis-gone-wrong out of their glasses). Before you know it, there'll be a whole lotta shakin' goin' on!

SISTERS' SECRETS TO CONFIDENT HOSTESSING

A smart solution for a glassware shortage

For this party, sexy stemmed martini glasses are part of the overall effect. Instead of stock-ing up on glasses that we might use only twice a year, here's our solution, one you can use for any party: Ask guests to show up with their own. It's a great little gimmick that gets guests into the spirit of the evening long before it arrives. We send out invitations cut in the shape of a martini glass and around the paper "stem," we tie an elegant black ribbon with the guest's name printed on the end with a silver pen. Along with the where-and-when details, the invite reads: "Please B.Y.O.G. You bring the glass, we'll keep it full of delicious drinks, this ribbon tied around its stem will ensure that it goes home with you at the end of the night." We've found that our guests happily oblige, and some take it as a challenge to bring the most unusual glasses they can find, which serve as one more Conversation Kick-Starter on party night.

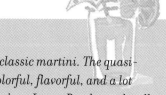

DESPITE THE NAME *of the party, we don't typically include the classic martini. The quasi-martinis we like to serve—we've given you our four favorites, below—are colorful, flavorful, and a lot more fun to mix up than the old gin-and-vermouth combo. But, hey, if you're a James Bond type, by all means include a bona fide martini. You can find a recipe in any cocktail book or on the Internet, though if you're truly in the 007 mold, you've got your own secret formula.*

PEAR-TINI

PEAR BRANDY IS *a little pricey, but this delicious cocktail is absolutely worth the cost.*

TO MAKE TWO DRINKS:

> **2 ounces vodka**
> **$\frac{1}{2}$ ounce orange-flavored vodka**
> **$\frac{1}{2}$ ounce pear brandy**
> **1 ounce lime juice**
> **$\frac{1}{2}$ ounce simple syrup**

SHAKE all the ingredients with ice and strain into a glass.

LEMON-TINI

THE BEAUTIFUL PALE *yellow color of this drink perfectly signals its light, fresh taste.*

TO MAKE TWO DRINKS:

> **3 ounces vodka**
> **2 ounces lemon juice**
> **$\frac{1}{2}$ ounce simple syrup**
> **$\frac{1}{2}$ ounce Cointreau or triple sec**
> **$\frac{1}{4}$ teaspoon orange bitters**

SHAKE all the ingredients with ice and strain into a glass.

BOURBON-TINI

THIS COULD ALSO *be called a cherry-tini. It's a gorgeous orangey-amber color and the bourbon and cherry give it a flavor almost like candy—but with a kick.*

TO MAKE TWO DRINKS:

> **$1\frac{1}{4}$ ounces vodka**
> **$1\frac{1}{4}$ ounces bourbon**
> **$1\frac{1}{4}$ ounces lemon juice**
> **$1\frac{1}{4}$ ounces maraschino cherry juice**
> **maraschino cherries**

SHAKE all the ingredients with ice and strain into a glass. Garnish with a cherry.

MAUI-TINI

FRUITY AND TROPICAL *without being overpower-ingly sweet.*

TO MAKE TWO DRINKS:

> **2 ounces vanilla-flavored vodka**
> **2 ounces pineapple juice**
> **1 ounce Rose's lime juice**
> **ground cinnamon (optional)**

SHAKE all the ingredients with ice and strain into a glass. For added visual appeal, dust the top of the drink with ground cinnamon.

THE MENU

With martinis, we recommend stomach-filling hors d'oeuvres.

Pork Tenderloin Sandwiches Two Ways

Seared Tuna and Cucumber Brochettes

Sun-dried Tomato and Ricotta Torte Trio

Fennel-Spiced Cauliflower Florets

Spiced Bar Nuts

RECIPES

pork tenderloin sandwiches two ways

MAKES ABOUT 45 SANDWICHES AND 1½ CUPS OF EACH MAYONNAISE

No one is happier than Anne's husband, RJ, when we serve these pork tenderloin sandwiches at our parties. They're the kind of hearty party food that men are always pleased to see on the table, and the choice of sandwich spreads gives guests a good excuse to go back for seconds.

FOR THE PORK TENDERLOIN

½ cup orange juice

¼ cup lime juice

¼ cup rum

1 medium onion, chopped

4 garlic cloves, minced

2 teaspoons ground cumin

2 teaspoons dried oregano

2 teaspoons salt

½ teaspoon ground black pepper

1 bay leaf, crumbled

3 pork tenderloins, about ¾ pound each

vegetable oil for oiling the pan

FOR THE APPLE-HORSERADISH MAYONNAISE

1 cup mayonnaise

½ cup applesauce, or more if you'd like to make the spread sweeter

3 tablespoons bottled horseradish

1½ teaspoons balsamic vinegar

salt and pepper

FOR THE RED CURRY MAYONNAISE

1½ cups mayonnaise

1 teaspoon prepared Thai red curry paste, or more to taste*

45 small bakery-bought sandwich rolls

PREPARE THE PORK: Combine all the ingredients except the vegetable oil in a large resealable plastic bag. Seal and turn the pork tenderloins in the bag until thoroughly coated with the marinade. Refrigerate at least 6 hours, or overnight.

PREHEAT oven to 350°F.

* *Most supermarkets we've looked in stock this near the soy sauce.*

TRANSFER the pork tenderloins to a lightly oiled baking pan, discarding the marinade. Roast until a thermometer inserted into the center of the pork registers about 140°F, 40 to 45 minutes. Remove from the oven and let stand 10 minutes (the pork's temperature will continue to rise to about 150°). Cut crosswise into ¼-inch slices.

PREPARE THE APPLE-HORSERADISH MAYONNAISE: Mix all the ingredients in a small bowl. Add salt and pepper to taste.

PREPARE THE RED CURRY MAYONNAISE: Mix all the ingredients in a small bowl.

SERVE THE PORK SLICES on a platter with a basket of rolls (slice them almost through before serving) and the two mayonnaises.

make-ahead factor: *The pork tenderloin can be marinated overnight. It can also be cooked 1 day ahead and kept covered and refrigerated. The mayonnaises may be made 3 to 4 days ahead and kept covered and refrigerated.*

seared tuna and cucumber brochettes

MAKES ABOUT 60 BROCHETTES

Seared tuna is one of those rare fish that taste just as good at room temperature as warm. In these easy-to-make skewers, the cool zip of the vinegared cucumber slices complements the tuna's luxurious taste and gives a nice texture contrast, too.

FOR THE TUNA

²/₃ cup extra-virgin olive oil

¹/₂ cup fresh lime juice

3 garlic cloves, minced

1 tablespoon chopped fresh thyme leaves

2 teaspoons grated fresh ginger

1¹/₂ pounds tuna steak, cut into ³/₄-inch cubes

FOR THE CUCUMBERS

2 tablespoons sugar

¹/₂ cup rice wine vinegar

1 large hothouse (seedless) cucumber, sliced in half lengthwise, then crosswise into thin slices

PREPARE THE TUNA: In a bowl, mix the olive oil, lime juice, garlic, thyme, and ginger. Add the tuna cubes, stir gently until all the cubes are coated, and let stand, covered, at room temperature for 15 minutes.

PREPARE THE CUCUMBERS: In a bowl, stir the sugar into the rice wine vinegar until dissolved. Add the cucumber slices and let them marinate for at least 15 minutes.

HEAT a large sauté pan over high heat until very hot but not smoking. Working in batches, use tongs to transfer the tuna pieces from the marinade to the pan and cook until browned on one side, 45 seconds to 1 minute. Then turn each cube to its opposite side and sear for the same amount of time. The tuna should still be rare.

TO MAKE EACH BROCHETTE, thread a cucumber slice onto a skewer or toothpick, then a piece of tuna. Arrange on a platter.

make-ahead factor: *The tuna cubes can be cooked 1 day ahead and kept covered and refrigerated. Let them come to room temperature before serving. The vinegared cucumbers can be made 1 day ahead (remove them from the marinade if keeping them longer than 1 hour) and kept covered and refrigerated. The assembled brochettes can be made 2 to 3 hours ahead and kept covered in plastic wrap on the serving tray.*

sun-dried tomato and ricotta torte trio

MAKES THREE 2-CUP TORTES

For these molded tortes, try using containers of three different shapes and heights to create a multi-tower sandcastle look. You can also give each individual torte its own look: we sometimes make dots or stripes with the first thin layer of sun-dried tomato (the one that will appear on the top of the torte when it's unmolded).

FOR THE SUN-DRIED TOMATO
MIXTURE

¾ cup chopped dried sun-dried tomatoes*

2 tablespoons olive oil

6 garlic cloves, minced

2 tablespoons balsamic vinegar

1½ teaspoons dried basil

¾ cup chopped fresh parsley

pepper

FOR THE RICOTTA MIXTURE

12 ounces cream cheese

¾ cup ricotta cheese

¾ cup (1½ sticks) butter

PREPARE THE TOMATO MIXTURE: Place the sun-dried tomatoes in a small bowl and add boiling water until just covered. Let stand until plumped, 10 to 15 minutes, then drain. Heat the olive oil in a skillet over medium heat. Add the tomatoes, garlic, balsamic vinegar, and basil. Cook for 1 minute. Remove from heat and stir in the parsley. Add pepper to taste.

PREPARE THE RICOTTA MIXTURE: Let all three ingredients come to room temperature in the bowl of a food processor. Process until smooth.

LINE THREE BOWLS, each with approximately a 2-cup capacity, with plastic wrap. Spoon enough sun-dried tomato mixture into one bowl to cover the bottom, then spoon in cheese mixture and smooth across the top until you have about a 1-inch layer. Add a 1-inch layer of tomato mixture and continue to alternate cheese and tomato until the bowl is full. Repeat with the other bowls. Cover tightly with plastic wrap and refrigerate until firm, about 4 hours.

* You can also use the sun-dried tomatoes that come packed in oil. Skip the step for rehydrating and reduce the olive oil by about half.

UNMOLD and bring to room temperature (this takes about an hour) before serving. Serve the tortes surrounded by crackers.

make-ahead factor: *Both mixtures can be made 2 days ahead and kept separately, tightly covered, in the refrigerator. You'll have to bring the ricotta mixture to room temperature again in order to spread it. The layered tortes can be made 1 day ahead and kept covered and refrigerated. Or you can make them up to 1 week ahead and freeze them in their bowls. Thaw at room temperature until the tortes can be unmolded, then continue to thaw until ready to serve.*

SISTERS' SECRETS TO CONFIDENT HOSTESSING

The ins and outs of ice

Ice is to parties as gasoline is to cars: you just can't run one without it, and when you use it all up, everything grinds to a halt. At this party in particular, where guests are shaking their own drinks, the fun lasts only as long as the ice does. Think about it: If your vodka supply dwindles, your guests will make gin drinks (believe us—we've seen it happen), but if you run out of ice, they'll start saying their good-byes. In our early party-throwing days, more than once we had to send someone out to the deli for more ice, so we started keeping track of how much we actually used. These guidelines should help:

- For a party where most of the drinks require ice (as does the Between the Sheets cocktail on page 45): 1 pound per person
- For a party where most people will drink wine or Champagne (such as the Champagne party on page 31 or the wine tasting on page 75): ½ pound per person, plus, if you're chilling the wine and Champagne on ice instead of in your refrigerator, ½ pound per bottle

- For this party, where lots of ice is needed for making the drinks: 2 pounds per person. Bottom line, though: Always, always buy more than you think you'll need. Ice is cheap. In the unlikely event that you have some left over, hey, it's only water going down the drain. Buy ice as close to party time as possible and keep what won't fit in the freezer in your bathtub or a cooler.

Note that we say ice is cheap, not free. That's because to make truly excellent cocktails, you need store-bought bagged ice. It's purer than anything a standard freezer can produce and therefore tastes far better. In a drink with lots of juice, that's not such a big deal, but with martini drinks, where you notice every little flavor, it's crucial. You can make ice cubes from filtered or bottled water, but why go to the trouble?

fennel-spiced cauliflower florets

MAKES ABOUT 6 CUPS OF CAULIFLOWER

This recipe was given to us by a family friend who often serves it at her own cocktail parties. She found it in the cookbook *Madhur Jaffrey's Indian Cooking*. The unusual spices turn plain cauliflower into a delicacy.

1 large cauliflower head	¼ teaspoon cayenne
7 tablespoons peanut oil	¼ teaspoon turmeric
1 tablespoon whole black mustard seeds	1 teaspoon salt
2 teaspoons whole fennel seeds	4 tablespoons water
2 to 3 garlic cloves, finely minced	

CUT THE CAULIFLOWER into bite-size florets. Put them in a bowl of cold water for at least half an hour and wait to drain until you're ready to cook them.

HEAT THE PEANUT OIL in a large skillet over medium heat. When the oil is hot, put in the mustard seeds and fennel seeds. As soon as the mustard seeds begin to pop, add the garlic. Cook, stirring frequently, until the garlic is lightly browned, 1 to 2 minutes. Add the cayenne and turmeric. Stir once to combine, then put in the cauliflower, salt, and water. Stir once, then cover the pan and cook 4 to 5 minutes.

REMOVE THE COVER and continue to cook until the liquid has evaporated and the cauliflower is cooked through but still slightly crisp, another 3 to 5 minutes. If the water evaporates before the cauliflower is cooked, add a little more.

SERVE warm or at room temperature with toothpicks.

make-ahead factor: *The cauliflower can be made 1 day ahead and kept covered and refrigerated. Bring it to room temperature before serving.*

spiced bar nuts

MAKES ABOUT 5 CUPS Of NUTS

We use pecans for this recipe because they're soft, almost meaty, and seem to soak up the spice mixture the best, but you can use any kind of nuts you like. Be sure to bake them long enough that they taste toasted, not raw. Place the nuts in bowls around the room.

2 tablespoons butter, melted	1 teaspoon onion salt
2 tablespoons finely chopped fresh rosemary	1 teaspoon Worcestershire sauce
2 teaspoons sugar	$1/4$ teaspoon Tabasco sauce
1 teaspoon garlic salt	$1/4$ teaspoon ground black pepper
	$1^1/4$ pounds fresh pecan halves

PREHEAT oven to 350°F.

IN A LARGE BOWL, combine the butter, rosemary, sugar, garlic salt, onion salt, Worcestershire sauce, hot sauce, and black pepper. Set aside.

SPREAD THE PECANS on a baking sheet and bake until they are lightly browned and cooked through, about 20 minutes. Add the warm nuts to the butter mixture and toss until thoroughly coated.

make-ahead factor: *The nuts can be made a week ahead and stored tightly covered.*

EVERYONE'S A LITTLE BIT PSYCHIC

You don't have to believe in astrology to get a kick out of reading your horoscope, and that principle prevails at this carnivalesque cocktail party. Even curmudgeons get swept up in the fun of crowd-pleasing, conversation-provoking "pseudo-psychic" pursuits such as palm-reading. And since the activities are quite literally hands-on, everybody gets familiar fast.

CONVERSATION
KICK-STARTER

The gist: At various places around the party, guests find simple instructions for conducting their own palm readings, handwriting analysis, and face reading. The stations have an undemanding, drop-in feel: Guests can work their way through them all or just stop for a minute to see what's going on.

The logistics: Decide on three areas in your house to set up stations for the activities. The supplies for each station are simple: For both palmistry and face reading, all you need is an instructional card showing guests the palm lines or facial features to look for. At the handwriting analysis table, supply guests with paper, pens, a copy of the text they will write out as a sample, plus the instructions for interpreting the results. On pages 101–5, we've supplied you with the table cards we used at one of our own Everyone's a Little Bit Psychic parties, and you can find tons of information on the Internet if you'd like to supplement our instructions or create your own. Remember, your goal is to get your party-goers to mingle, not to actually predict their futures. The emphasis should be on fun and collaboration, so don't stress out over creating elaborate set-ups. You just need a few fun examples to make guests loosen up and laugh.

LIFE LINE

THE LIFE LINE *begins on the edge of the palm, between the index finger and the thumb. It extends across the middle of the palm and wraps around the base of the thumb.*

This line is an index of your vitality, strength, and energy.

> *Line runs close to your thumb: You're low-energy.* Your idea of a good time is a midday nap.
>
> vs.
>
> *Line curves wide toward the center of your palm: You're high-energy.* You like to party all night.

> *The line reaches to the base of your palm:* You will have a long and healthy life.
>
> vs.
>
> *The line stops short of the base of your palm:* Well, not to be the bearer of bad news, but . . .

> *Double or triple lines:* Good news! Extra lines are called "vitality lines." You will not lose your hair. You will not need Viagra.

READ YOUR PALM

HEAD LINE

THE HEAD LINE *begins just above the life line, on the side of the palm between the thumb and the index finger, and crosses the palm horizontally, generally ending under your ring finger.*

This line deals with your beliefs and your philosophy, as well as memory, intelligence, and reasoning.

Short vs. long: Short-liners often jump to conclusions. A long head line shows you are a person who thinks things through very carefully.

Head line joined to life line at the beginning: Your mind rules over your body. Are you a lawyer?

vs.

Head line separate from life line: Your love of adventure sometimes overrules your logical impulses. Remember that swimming-with-the-sharks incident?

Double lines: You may be Mensa material.

Short line curved upwards: You're almost certainly a scatterbrain.

Wavy line: You may not have read this far due to your short attention span.

HEART LINE

THE HEART LINE *is the horizontal line above the head line. It generally begins beneath the index finger or middle finger and extends to the edge of the palm on the side of the little finger.*

This line rules your emotions and relationships. In general, the stronger and deeper the line, the stronger and warmer your heart.

Line starts below the middle finger: You're a romantic. You recite poetry and send roses.

vs.

Starts beneath the index finger: You're prosaic about love. You think a George Foreman grill is a great anniversary gift.

vs.

Starts between the middle and index finger: You tend to go overboard when it comes to relationships. You don't just declare your love, you tattoo it on your arm.

Line extends across the entire palm: You lose yourself in your significant other. He plays golf, you play golf. He likes old Kojak movies, you shave your head.

vs.

Line ends before the edge of your palm: You're independent even when you're part of a couple. In fact, you haven't seen your significant other since the two of you arrived tonight.

ANALYZE YOUR HANDWRITING

Please write the following line (a quote from Alexander Woollcott) on the provided pad. Don't think about it too hard, and don't try to be extra-neat.

All the things I really like to do are either illegal, immoral or fattening.

the slant: Does your handwriting slant toward the right, left, or is it upright?

Slanted to the right: You are an outward-directed person, focusing on others and on the outside world rather than yourself.

Slanted to the left: You are an inward-directed person with an emphasis on yourself and an attachment to the past. You are also resistant to change.

Straight up and down: You are self-reliant and self-disciplined. You possess great poise and are grounded in the present.

Slanted both ways: You have trouble making up your mind.

the t-bar: Do you cross your t's neatly or not at all?

Bar crosses the "t": You are neat and tidy both in your handwriting and your personal life. You like things to be organized and can't stand messy relationships.

Bar misses the upright of the "t": You are a free spirit. Anyone who tries to get you riled up will be disappointed. You are at peace with yourself.

No bar at all: You are not one to let your head get in the way of a good time. You are spontaneous to a fault.

the i-dot: Do you dot your i's neatly?

Dot right above i: You are a perfectionist with a keen attention to detail. Some would call you stubborn.

Dot falls to the right of the i: You are a forward-thinker who sometimes loses touch with reality.

Dot falls to the left of the i: You are a cautious person, slow to make decisions but a good secret-keeper.

the m-humps: Are the humps in your m's symmetrical?

Humps are equal height: You are reserved, almost secretive, and unlikely to be controlled by your emotions.

Second hump is higher: You are a loyal and dedicated friend renowned for your sense of justice.

Second hump is lower: You love challenges and have very strong willpower. You don't let anyone get in your way.

WHAT DOES YOUR FACE SAY ABOUT YOU?

the distance between your eyes

One eye-width between your eyes is a sign of balanced judgment and a clear view of the world. You are a good sport.

Eyes set closer than one eye-width apart indicate that you have a calculating approach to life and are very opinionated. You are a perfectionist.

Eyes set farther than one eye-width apart indicate that you are very tolerant of others and unconcerned by new and challenging situations. You can also be a bit too gullible.

floating irises

White is visible under the iris of the eye. This indicates inner turbulence. You are at odds with the world and may feel misunderstood. You share this trait with Princess Diana and Michael Jackson.

White is visible above the iris of the eye. This indicates dangerous personality elements, perhaps an explosive temper. Charles Manson had these eyes!

earlobes

If your earlobes are attached, you are independent and know what you want out of life.

If your earlobes are not attached, you are creative type with a seeking nature.

GUESTS DRINK *one glass of this potent potion and find they're blessed with the gift of gab. Two glasses in, they develop amazing powers of persuasion. On glass three, they're mind-readers—hence the name.*

EVERYONE'S-A-LITTLE-BIT-PSYCHIC SANGRIA

TO MAKE A PITCHER (ABOUT 20 DRINKS):

- 1.5 liters red wine
- 1 cup rum
- ½ can frozen limeade or pink lemonade concentrate
- 1½ cups orange juice
- 1 cup lemon-lime soda or collins mixer

YOU CAN COMBINE all the ingredients except the lemon-lime soda a day in advance and keep the sangria refrigerated. Add the soda no more than an hour before the party. To serve, pour the sangria into ice-filled glasses and garnish each with orange and lime slices, if desired.

THE MENU

Delicious food with a touch of the exotic

Peppery Shrimp

Asian Chicken Meatballs with Sweet-Sour Sauce

Cucumber Goat Cheese Spread

Crudités with Carrot-Ginger Dip

Fortune Cookies

RECIPES

peppery shrimp

MAKES ABOUT 50 SHRIMP

These richly spiced shrimp are an elegant improvement on the traditional chilled boiled presentation—and are so flavorful that they need no sauce.

½ cup Dijon mustard

½ cup extra-virgin olive oil, plus more for cooking

½ cup white wine vinegar

¼ cup minced celery

¼ cup minced shallots

¼ cup minced parsley

4 teaspoons crushed red pepper, or more for greater spice

1½ teaspoons salt

2 pounds large shrimp, peeled and deveined, leaving tails on for "handles"

COMBINE ALL THE INGREDIENTS in a large resealable plastic bag, shake once or twice to make sure the shrimp are coated, and marinate in the refrigerator for 4 to 6 hours.

DRAIN THE SHRIMP into a sieve and shake to drain off excess marinade. Coat a large skillet with olive oil and heat over medium heat. Place the shrimp in one layer (don't crowd them—if necessary, cook the shrimp in two batches). Cook, shaking the pan occasionally to turn the shrimp, until the shrimp turn pink and are cooked through, 3 to 5 minutes. They can be served warm or at room temperature.

make-ahead factor: *The marinade can be prepared up to 2 days ahead and kept covered and refrigerated. The cooked shrimp can be made the morning of the party and kept covered and refrigerated. Bring them to room temperature before serving.*

asian chicken meatballs with sweet-sour sauce

MAKES ABOUT 40 MEATBALLS AND 1 CUP OF SAUCE

Water chestnuts add a nice little crunch to these mouth-watering meatballs, and the sauce has that wonderful Asian quality of being sweet, tangy, and savory all at the same time.

FOR THE MEATBALLS

$^1\!/_2$ cup (about 4 ounces) water chestnuts, drained and rinsed with cold water

$^1\!/_4$ cup chopped shallots

$^1\!/_2$ teaspoon chopped jalapeño pepper

$^1\!/_2$ teaspoon grated fresh ginger

1 garlic clove

$^1\!/_2$ pound ground chicken

$^3\!/_4$ cup fine fresh bread crumbs (1–2 slices white bread, ground in food processor)

2 teaspoons soy sauce

1 teaspoon cornstarch

1 teaspoon oyster sauce

1 teaspoon rice wine vinegar

$^1\!/_4$ teaspoon salt

$^1\!/_4$ teaspoon ground black pepper

peanut oil for cooking

FOR THE SWEET-SOUR SAUCE

2 tablespoons toasted sesame oil

2 garlic cloves, minced

3 teaspoons ground coriander

$^1\!/_2$ teaspoon ground cinnamon

$^1\!/_4$ teaspoon grated nutmeg

$^1\!/_2$ cup water

4 tablespoons oyster sauce

$^1\!/_4$ teaspoon grated lime zest

5 tablespoons lime juice

2 tablespoons soy sauce

2 tablespoons sherry

2 teaspoons sugar

2 teaspoons cornstarch mixed with 2 teaspoons cold water

PREPARE THE MEATBALLS: In a food processor, pulse the water chestnuts, shallots, jalapeño pepper, ginger, and garlic until finely ground. Transfer the mixture to a large bowl. Add the chicken and all the remaining ingredients except the peanut oil. Mix gently just until combined (the mixture will be fairly wet). Form into 1-inch balls, placing them on a plate or baking sheet (they can be close together, but not touching). Chill the meatballs in the refrigerator for at least 30 minutes to firm up.

LIGHTLY COAT A LARGE SKILLET with peanut oil and heat over medium heat until the oil is hot. Put as many meatballs in the skillet as will fit without touching and cook for 3 to 4 minutes, until the bottoms of the meatballs are browned and they release easily from the pan's surface. Then, with a spatula or by gently shaking the pan, stir the meatballs, let them cook another minute, stir again, and repeat until they are browned all over and cooked through, 6 to 8 minutes total.

PREPARE THE SAUCE: Heat the sesame oil in a small saucepan. Add the garlic, coriander, cinnamon, and nutmeg, and cook until the garlic is lightly browned, 2 to 3 minutes. Remove the pan from the heat and add the water, oyster sauce, lime zest, lime juice, soy sauce, sherry, and sugar. Stir. Return the pan to the heat and bring to a boil. Simmer for 2 minutes. Add the cornstarch and water mixture and cook, stirring constantly, for another 2 to 3 minutes, until the sauce is slightly thickened. Set aside.

SERVE THE MEATBALLS warm with the sauce alongside (the sauce is just as good at room temperature as warm). Provide toothpicks.

make-ahead factor: *The meatballs can be frozen, uncooked, up to 1 week ahead. Thaw completely in the refrigerator and cook as directed. They can also be cooked the morning of the party and kept covered and refrigerated. Warm them in a 350°F oven before serving. The sauce can be made up to 1 week ahead and kept covered and refrigerated. It can be warmed in the microwave.*

cucumber goat cheese spread

MAKES ABOUT 1¼ CUPS OF SPREAD

This recipe from *Gourmet* has been in our clipping collection for nearly 10 years, and it's always been a hit, even with guests who think they don't like goat cheese. Tarragon's subtle hint of licorice gives the spread an interesting flavor that people invariably ask about.

1 hothouse (seedless) cucumber, peeled, seeded, and finely chopped (about 1½ cups)

8 ounces soft mild goat cheese

1½ teaspoons grated fresh lemon zest

1½ teaspoons fresh lemon juice

2 tablespoons finely chopped red onion

2 teaspoons finely chopped fresh tarragon leaves

½ teaspoon freshly ground black pepper

salt

IN A FOOD PROCESSOR, puree 1 cup of the cucumber with the goat cheese, lemon zest, and lemon juice until almost smooth. In a bowl, stir together the goat-cheese mixture, remaining cucumber, 1 tablespoon of onion, tarragon, and the pepper. Add salt to taste. Garnish with the remaining tablespoon of onion and serve with slices of soft, crusty bread.

make-ahead factor: *The spread maybe made 2 days ahead and kept covered and refrigerated. Let the spread soften and stir it before serving.*

crudités with carrot-ginger dip

This dip was inspired by the carrot-ginger salad dressing served at sushi restaurants. The fresh, tangy flavor and slightly crunchy mouth feel make a nice change from creamy dips and, in this party, contrast nicely with the richer goat cheese spread.

½ pound carrots (about 3 medium), peeled	2 tablespoons rice vinegar
¼ cup chopped shallot (1 large)	1 tablespoon toasted sesame oil
2 tablespoons chopped fresh ginger	1½ teaspoons soy sauce
	¼ cup peanut oil

CUT THE CARROTS into 1-inch pieces and pulse in a food processor until finely ground but not quite pureed. Add the shallot, ginger, vinegar, sesame oil, and soy sauce and pulse until the ginger and shallot are minced and combined with the carrots.

WITH THE FOOD PROCESSOR ON, pour in the peanut oil in a stream. Continue to process a few seconds more to make sure all ingredients are thoroughly combined. Transfer the mixture to a fine-meshed sieve set over a bowl and let drain for 30 to 45 minutes or until no more liquid is coming through the sieve.

SERVE with crudités. (See page 28 for hints on how to prepare them.)

make-ahead factor: *The dip can be made 2 days ahead and kept covered and refrigerated. Take it out of the refrigerator 30 minutes before serving; the flavors are best when the dip is not overly chilled.*

fortune cookies

Fortune cookies, offered in bowls around the room, are a conversation-sparker in themselves. Reading the fortunes aloud is almost a requirement. We always have a lot of fun with these, creating quirky messages like "You will not find a gray hair for at least another two weeks" or "Kiss the nearest woman and good fortune will smile upon you."

FOR THE FORTUNES

Printing these out on a computer is the quickest way to create lots of fortunes. Cut each slip about 3/8 inch wide and 2 1/2 inches long (so the ends stick out slightly from the cookies).

FOR THE COOKIES

2/3 cup sifted cake flour

2/3 cup granulated sugar

4 large egg whites

4 tablespoons confectioners' sugar

4 tablespoons canola oil

2 tablespoons butter, softened

2 teaspoons pure vanilla extract

large pinch salt

vegetable oil for oiling the pan

PREHEAT oven to 300°F.

IN A FOOD PROCESSOR, combine all of the ingredients except the vegetable oil and process until smooth. Drop 6 scant tablespoonfuls of the batter onto a lightly oiled baking sheet. (Set the remaining batter aside.) With a small spatula or the back of a spoon, spread each spoonful into a 3 3/4-inch circle. Bake until quite golden, 10 to 15 minutes.

HAVE A SMALL BOWL and a muffin tin ready. Remove the baking sheet from the oven. With a thin spatula, carefully loosen the cookies but leave them on the baking sheet. Return the sheet of cookies to the oven to keep them warm and pliable. Remove one cookie at a time from the oven. Lay a fortune in the center and roll the cookie into a tube, overlapping the edges slightly. Holding the ends, with the "seam" side down, fold the cookie in half over the rim of the bowl to form the traditional fortune cookie shape. Immediately transfer the cookie to the muffin tin to keep it from opening up as it cools. Repeat with the remaining cookies.

SPREAD AND BAKE the remaining batter and form cookies as directed above.

LOW EFFORT: You can buy fortune cookies online or from your local Chinese restaurant, though of course you won't be able to control the fortunes.

make-ahead factor: *The cookies can be baked 1 day ahead and kept tightly covered.*

How to get an accurate head count

Sometimes, we feel as though instead of the gentle French formality of "RSVP," our invitations should read LUKWYCD—Let us know whether you're coming, damnit! Unfortunately, among any group of guests, there are bound to be some RSVP shirkers. We forgive them for their wayward ways, but there are hors d'oeuvres to prepare and liquor to buy—we need a *somewhat* accurate head count. Plus, not knowing whether you'll have a full house sets off that nagging little fear that every hostess harbors: "What if *nobody* comes?"

Luckily, the ubiquity of e-mail has cut down on RSVP shirkage. Always provide your e-mail address along with your phone number for responses. When we invited nearly 60 people to a party we threw for our mother's birthday, the only reply that came via the phone was from our grandmother— and encouragingly, we heard from 90 percent of the invitees without having to nudge. When we provide a phone number only, the response rate is more like 75 percent. (We're talking about how many get back to us, not how many accept the invitation—there's info on that on page 14.)

The other great thing about e-mail is that it feels more casual than a phone call, so you can nudge the shirkers with a gentle reminder note without being ill-mannered yourself. Use a light touch with the language—you're just finalizing the guest list and are soooo hoping they'll be there—so that instead of feeling singled out or scolded, the shirker feels extra-desirable. You'll almost always get a response.

THE RISKY BUSINESS BASH

There's something irresistible about quizzes. Whether it's "Are you a flirt?" or "Do you watch too much TV?" everyone loves the idea of rating himself, and half the fun is sharing your score. In this party, guests discover their Daredevil Level, based on how many of a list of adventurous activities they can say they've done: bungee-jumped, sky-dived, been arrested, eaten brains—you can tailor the list to your audience. *You* try meeting somebody who's tried 9 out of 10 things and not asking which one didn't make the cut. Impossible!

CONVERSATION
KICK-STARTER

The gist: Hang or prop a small poster with the risky business checklist in a prominent place in the room. Guests will gather around it and mentally work through the list, tallying the number of risky behaviors they've participated in. Depending on their score, they get either an orange "high-risk" sticker or a white "low-risk" sticker to put on their clothes or cocktail glass (which makes for an ice-breaker when guests migrate back toward the rest of the party). The whole process sparks tale-trading, eyebrow-raising, and lots of high-fiving and woo-hooing.

The logistics: At the top of the poster, indicate what guests should do with language like this:

RATE YOUR DAREDEVIL LEVEL

GIVE YOURSELF ONE POINT FOR EACH OF THE FOLLOWING RISKY THINGS YOU'VE DONE

Then make up your checklist, borrowing from our master list or coming up with your own—we generally keep the list to 10 to 12 entries to avoid audience fatigue. You can adjust the risky activities to suit your crowd: for a more sedate group of guests, you might include "kissed a total stranger" and leave off "had a one-night stand," for instance. Or, what the hell, be an agent provocateur. Being a little outrageous makes a party memorable. As Elsa Maxwell, a renowned Hollywood hostess in the '30s and '40s, once advised: "Serve the dinner backward, do anything. But for goodness sake, do something weird."

Beside the poster, place sheets of small stickers in two colors, a felt-tip pen, and a small sign that says something along the lines of:

A SCORE OF 6 OR HIGHER
You are somewhere between risk-tolerant and having a death wish.
Please write your score on an orange sticker.

A SCORE OF 5 OR LOWER:
You are somewhere between moderately risk-averse and absolute milquetoast.
Please write your score on a white sticker.

TO GET YOU STARTED: A RISKY BUSINESS CHECKLIST

Give yourself one point if you've . . .

1. Kissed a total stranger
2. Eaten the worm at the bottom of a bottle of mezcal
3. Joined the Mile-High Club
4. Flashed your boobs (if you're a woman) or mooned someone (either sex)
5. Streaked
6. Had a one-night stand
7. Crashed a party
8. Objected at a wedding
9. Lied about your age or occupation to get a date
10. Driven a car at over 100 mph
11. Drunk the H2O in Mexico
12. Kayaked/rafted/canoed in rapids of any class over 3
13. Let your coworkers see a picture of you from junior high
14. Skinny-dipped in daylight
15. Sunbathed nude at a public beach
16. Bungee-jumped
17. Skydived or hang-glided
18. Handled a snake
19. Gone on a blind date set up by your mother or grandmother
20. Eaten any kind of insect (or brains or whatever suits your crowd)
21. Done stand-up comedy
22. Swallowed a sword, walked on hot coals, ridden a bicycle on a tightrope, or any other bona fide circus/carnival act
23. Had a baby without pain-killing drugs
24. Shoplifted
25. Been arrested

It's also fun to provide a fill-in-the-blank space on the poster for guests to jot down the crazy behaviors they've tried that you haven't asked them about (anonymously, if they choose!).

OUR MOTHER'S POWERFUL *margaritas are legendary among her friends, our friends, and all of our friends' friends. These aren't the wimpy, sour-mixy margaritas you may know from restaurants; they're as pure as a margarita gets. Drink them at your own risk!*

MICHELE'S KILLER MARGARITAS

TO MAKE ONE DRINK:

> 3/4 ounce fresh lime juice
>
> coarse salt
>
> 2 ounces Cuervo Gold tequila*
>
> 1 1/4 ounces triple sec

MOISTEN THE RIM OF A GLASS with lime juice, then coat with salt. Shake all the ingredients vigorously with ice for 20 seconds and strain into the salted, ice-filled glass.

TO MAKE A PITCHER (ABOUT 20 DRINKS):

> 5 cups tequila
>
> 3 cups plus 2 tablespoons triple sec
>
> 1 3/4 cups plus 2 tablespoons fresh lime juice
>
> coarse salt

COMBINE all the ingredients except the salt in a large pitcher, add ice, and stir vigorously for about 30 seconds. Spoon out the ice cubes. Store the pitcher in the refrigerator until party time. Serve in glasses with salted rims.

---

* *If you consider yourself a margarita fan, you may be tempted to go "top shelf" on us and substitute some fancy tequila for the Cuervo. Don't. We've tried this drink with several premium tequilas, and though the resulting drinks were good, they didn't have the just-rough-enough limey perfection of Michele's. And these are easier on the wallet.*

THE MENU

This party's about risk-taking, but the food's a sure bet.

Empanaditas

Goat Cheese and Leek Croustades

Artichoke and Green Olive Dip

Creamy Crab Dip with Jicama Spears

Pistachios

Recipes

empanaditas

MAKES ABOUT 50 EMPANADITAS

Traditionally, these little meat turnovers are made with pastry dough. Using wonton wrappers is quicker and easier, and makes for a pleasingly crispy shell.

FOR THE FILLING

1 tablespoon canola oil, plus more for frying

1/2 cup finely chopped green bell pepper

1/2 cup minced onion

1/2 pound fresh chorizo (casing removed), chopped*

2 small garlic cloves, minced

1/2 teaspoon ground cumin

salt and pepper

FOR THE WRAPPERS

1 package wonton wrappers (approximately 50)

1 egg, lightly beaten for an egg wash

PREPARE THE FILLING: Heat 1 tablespoon of the oil in a saucepan over medium heat. Add the bell pepper and onion and cook, stirring, until softened. Add the garlic and cook for an additional 2 minutes, then add the sausage and cumin. Cook until the sausage is brown and thoroughly cooked through, 5 to 7 minutes. Add salt and pepper to taste.

PREPARE THE EMPANADITAS: Using a 3-inch cookie cutter, cut a round out of each wonton wrapper. Place a teaspoon of the sausage mixture in the middle of each round. Dab the egg wash around the edges, using your finger or a pastry brush. Fold it over, forming a semi-circle, and press the tines of a fork into the edges to seal them and create a decorative border. After assembling, refrigerate the uncooked empanaditas for about 20 minutes before cooking.

* Chopping uncooked sausage can be a little difficult. If large pieces remain after cooking, simply chop the cooked sausage mixture to make it easier to fill the wrappers.

TO COOK, cover the bottom of a large saucepan with canola oil and heat over medium-high heat. When the oil is hot, add enough empanaditas to fill the pan without touching (they should sizzle when added to the pan). Cook 3 to 4 minutes on one side, then turn and continue cooking for another 2 minutes or until well-browned on both sides. Remove from pan and drain on paper towels.

CONTINUE COOKING IN BATCHES, keeping the cooked empanaditas on a baking tray in a 200°F oven to stay warm. Serve warm.

make-ahead factor: *The sausage filling can be made up to 2 days ahead and kept covered and refrigerated. The empanaditas can be assembled and frozen, uncooked, in single layers separated by plastic wrap, for up to 1 week. Thaw fully in the refrigerator, then cook according to the recipe.*

goat cheese and leek croustades

MAKES 36 CROUSTADES

Of all the edible containers we use for hors d'oeuvres, these are the easiest to make. Use the highest-quality white bread you can find (this is not the time for Wonder Bread).

FOR THE CROUSTADE CUPS

36 slices high-quality white sandwich bread*

4 tablespoons (½ stick) butter, melted

FOR THE FILLING

1 tablespoon butter

1 cup finely chopped leeks, white and pale green parts (about 2 medium leeks)

8 ounces soft mild goat cheese

3 tablespoons plain yogurt

2 tablespoons chopped parsley

1½ tablespoons finely chopped chives

1 tablespoon extra-virgin olive oil

¼ teaspoon salt

⅛ teaspoon freshly ground pepper

¼ cup pine nuts

PREHEAT oven to 350°F.

PREPARE THE CUPS: With a 2½-inch round cookie cutter, cut out a round of bread from each slice. Brush one side of each round with the melted butter. Press the bread, butter side down, into the cup of a mini muffin tin. The bread will not reach the top of the cups. Bake until the top edges are browned, 11 to 13 minutes. Remove the croustades to a wire rack to cool. Keep the oven at 350°F.

PREPARE THE FILLING: In a large saucepan, melt the butter over low to medium heat. Add the leeks and sauté, stirring frequently, until softened, 8 to 10 minutes. If the leeks begin to brown, lower the heat.

IN A FOOD PROCESSOR, blend the goat cheese, yogurt, parsley, chives, olive oil, salt, and pepper until smooth. Transfer to a bowl and stir in leeks. Set aside.

* *Our favorite white bread is small, so we can only get one round per slice. If you use a larger loaf, you may be able to cut two rounds from each slice and will only need 18 slices.*

TOAST THE PINE NUTS in a small pan over medium heat, shaking frequently, until lightly browned, 5 to 7 minutes. Set aside.

RETURN THE CROUSTADE CUPS to the muffin tins and fill each cup with goat cheese mixture. Top with 3 to 4 pine nuts. Bake for about 5 minutes.

make-ahead factor: *The croustade cups can be made 3 days ahead and kept tightly covered at room temperature. The goat cheese filling can be made 3 days ahead and kept covered and refrigerated. The assembled croustades can be made and baked, then frozen for up to 2 weeks. Warm them in a 350°F oven for 12 to 15 minutes. With a metal spatula, remove the croustades to a wire rack for a few minutes until the cups firm up.*

How to know if you should hire outside help

Our party-throwing philosophy is based on being able to do everything ourselves, but even we have occasionally looked at each other in a moment of pre-party frenzy—when the guest list has ballooned from 25 to 40, or we've decided to entertain on short notice—and said, "We could use some help here!" Hired hands can be a lifesaver for a busy host, but be aware that there are pros and cons. We talked to party-throwing friends who frequently arrange for professional help—as well as the pros themselves—to create these whom-to-hire guidelines:

CATERER

PROS: You can hire a chef/caterer to prepare the hors d'oeuvres in your kitchen from recipes you provide, so the menu still has your personal stamp.

CONS: This is generally the most expensive help to hire since it requires the greatest skill. Plus, this is not the option for control freaks, since caterers generally like to have the kitchen to themselves.

BARTENDER

PROS: All the during-the-evening chores associated with the bar are taken care of for you: ice is replenished, pitchers refilled, empty glasses collected, etc.

CONS: A do-it-yourself bar is one of the social centers of a cocktail party—and especially at the parties in this book, which always include a conversation-spurring signature cocktail and sometimes make the drink-mixing a major component of the evening. Installing a bartender lends an air of formality that can make guests feel pampered, but can also put a damper on the fun.

KITCHEN HELP

PROS: This is the most versatile help to hire: he or she can assist with cooking and set-up before guests arrive, can keep the hors d'oeuvres coming from the kitchen while you're mingling in the living room, and can get a jump on the clean-up as the party winds down.

CONS: A jack-of-all-trades helper needs more instruction than a one-task bartender or chef. You'll need to think through the tasks you want done, explain each one in detail, and probably check in with the helper throughout the party.

NEXT-DAY CLEANING HELP

PROS: You go to bed aglow with the success of your evening, blithely ignoring the dirty glasses and the pistachio shells that have found their way under the sofa. No need to worry—tomorrow morning, help arrives to restore your house to order while you loll on the sofa receiving thank-you phone calls from delighted guests.

CONS: You go to bed aglow with the success of your evening—and perhaps one too many margaritas—and the next day the cleaning help sweeps in at the crack of dawn, clanking plates and running the noisy dishwasher just when you could use a nice morning in bed.

artichoke and green olive dip

MAKES ABOUT 3 CUPS OF DIP

Both of us love artichokes—steamed and eaten with melted butter, chilled and dipped in lemon mayonnaise, or blended with all manner of other ingredients for delicious dips. This dip has an unusual flavor and a beautiful pale green color.

2 (14.5-ounce) cans whole artichoke hearts

½ cup extra-virgin olive oil

2 teaspoons fresh lemon juice

2 garlic cloves, minced

1 cup pitted green olives, finely chopped pepper

¼ cup finely chopped fresh parsley

DRAIN THE ARTICHOKE HEARTS and rinse them in cool water. Pat them dry with paper towels and place them in a food processor with the olive oil, lemon juice, and garlic. Puree until smooth, 2 to 3 minutes. Transfer the puree to a bowl and stir in the green olives. Add pepper to taste (the dip should already be pretty salty from the green olives). Chill for at least 2 hours. Before serving, stir in the chopped parsley.

LOW EFFORT: Serve with crackers, breadsticks, or corn chips.

MO' EFFORT: Serve with toasted pita triangles and endive leaves.

make-ahead factor: *The dip can be made up to 2 days ahead and kept covered and refrigerated.*

creamy crab dip with jicama spears

MAKES ABOUT 3 CUPS OF DIP

We served this crab dip at our first New Year's Eve party in New York City. Lauren's handwritten note on the recipe is "monster hit." It has appeared at many parties since.

FOR THE CRAB DIP

2 (8-ounce) packages cream cheese, softened

1¼ pounds lump crabmeat, drained and picked over to remove any shell, then shredded*

4 tablespoons grated onion

1 tablespoon prepared horseradish

1 tablespoon Worcestershire sauce

2 teaspoons lemon juice

1½ teaspoons Tabasco sauce, or to taste

1 garlic clove, finely minced

1 teaspoon ground cumin

¼ teaspoon white pepper

FOR THE JICAMA

1 large jicama, pared**

juice of 1 lime

2–3 teaspoons ground cumin

PREPARE THE DIP: Beat the cream cheese in a large bowl with an electric mixer until creamy. Stir in the crabmeat, then the rest of the ingredients. Microwave the dip in the bowl for about a minute, or until heated through. Stir again.

PREPARE THE JICAMA: Cut the pared jicama into square-sided spears (think of the shape of thick-cut french fries). In a bowl, toss them with enough lime juice to lightly coat. Drain on paper towels or use a paper towel to blot off excess juice, then sprinkle liberally with cumin.

PUT THE JICAMA on a serving plate and serve the dip alongside.

MO' EFFORT: Create a bread bowl by hollowing out a large round loaf of Italian or sourdough bread. Cut the bread you removed from the bowl into chunks, drizzle

* *We've also successfully used high-quality canned crabmeat in this recipe. It, too, needs to be picked over to remove shell pieces.*
** *The best way to pare this somewhat intimidating vegetable: Cut it in half crosswise. Set one half cut side down on a cutting board and, starting from the top, cut down toward the cutting board, slicing fairly deeply to get through the thick skin. Work in strips around the circumference. Repeat with the other half.*

with olive oil, and sprinkle with salt. Put the bowl on a baking sheet, toss the bread chunks around it, and bake until lightly toasted in the oven. Fill the bowl with crab mixture and put the extra bread out with the jicama. (Don't forget to add serving spoons or spreaders if you're using bread chunks; they're not as easy to dip by hand as the jicama spears.)

make-ahead factor: *The jicama can be cut, tossed with lime juice, and kept covered and refrigerated for 1 day. Sprinkle on the cumin just before serving. The crab dip can be made 3 days ahead and kept covered and refrigerated. Bring to room temperature before serving.*

pistachios

Mound salted pistachios (with shells on) in bowls around the party space—we like the California jumbo variety. If we have time, we pick through the nuts and discard the ones that are closed so tightly there's no hope of ever cracking them. Provide a discard bowl for shells next to every bowl of nuts.

your anti-stress kit:
the flexible party-planning timeline

No matter how casual or impromptu the party, the key to success—and sanity—is to have a schedule. We've both got jobs, so we have to fit our party-prep in on weekends, lunch hours, and after work. To execute each party with maximum efficiency and minimum panic, we create a written list of every-thing we need to get done and when we plan to fit it in. Below, you'll see how we pulled together the Risky Business party on a Saturday night. Obviously, your plan won't look exactly like ours, but this should help you check off all your chores so that when guests show up, you're the hostess with the mostest, not the almostest.

WEEKEND BEFORE THE PARTY

✔ **GROCERY SHOP.** All the food for this party can be bought a week ahead, even the leeks for the croustades and fresh chorizo sausage for the empanaditas since we're making those recipes ahead.

✔ **COOK.** Take advantage of freezable hors d'oeuvres that can be made a full week or more ahead; in this case, we make the empanaditas and goat cheese-leek croustades.

MONDAY

✔ **MAKE THE RISKY BUSINESS LIST.** We e-mail back and forth during down moments at the office until we have a list we love.

✔ **BUY PARTY SUPPLIES.** On our lunch hour we pick up poster board, stickers, and lots of cocktail napkins. Both of us have plans in the evening, but no big deal—we've already got the two most time-consuming hors d'oeuvres taken care of.

TUESDAY

✔ **NEATEN UP THE APARTMENT AFTER WORK.** Don't forget to stock the guest bathroom with extra rolls of toilet paper.

✔ **CHOOSE MUSIC.** We're fans of premixed CDs (see page 25), but for this party, we're burning our own CD because every tenth song or so we want to insert the theme music from Mission: Impossible.

✔ **COUNT AND WASH GLASSWARE.** This is an easy task while watching TV. We make a note to buy or borrow five more glasses.

WEDNESDAY

✔ **BUY MORE GLASSES.** Lunch-hour trip to Crate & Barrel.

✔ **MAKE CRAB DIP.** Easy! It takes only 20 minutes out of our evening.

THURSDAY

It's a crazy work day, so we have no lunch-hour freedom at all. But our evening is free:

✔ **GET OUT TRAYS AND BOWLS.** Decide which hors d'oeuvres will be served on each.

✔ **MAKE ARTICHOKE AND GREEN OLIVE DIP.**

✔ **CREATE THE RISKY BUSINESS POSTER.**

FRIDAY

We sneak out of our offices by 5:

✔ **MAKE ONE LAST SHOPPING TRIP.** We buy drink mixers like club soda and tonic; sodas for non-drinking guests; limes and lemons for drink garnishes; and more crab dip ingredients since we've eaten half of the dip since Wednesday!

✔ **CUT JICAMA TO GO WITH CRAB DIP.**

✔ **ORDER LIQUOR TO BE DELIVERED.** Buy extra tequila since margaritas are the signature cocktail.

✔ **SET UP THE BUFFET TABLE.** We decide to use a hotplate for the empanaditas and maybe for the crab dip. Everything else can be served at room temperature.

✔ **DIG OUT THE NUMBER FOR A CAR SERVICE.** Put it on the fridge where guests can find it.

✔ **SET UP A COLLAPSIBLE COAT RACK.** (Or we just let guests throw their coats on the sofa in the spare room.)

✔ **PUT UP THE RISKY BUSINESS POSTER.** Don't forget stickers and pens.

SATURDAY MORNING

✔ **FIRST THINGS FIRST.** Pedicures!

✔ **PLACE VOTIVE CANDLES AROUND THE ROOM.** That's our answer to decorating (see page 79).

✔ **ALLERGIC FRIEND ALERT.** Move the cat's food and water bowls into the bedroom so he can be shut in during the party.

SATURDAY AFTERNOON/EARLY EVENING

✔ **BUY ICE.**

✔ **LAST-MINUTE RECIPE STUFF.** Cut pita triangles to go with the artichoke-green olive dip; put the pistachios in bowls; cut limes and lemons into wedges for cocktail garnishes. Make several pitchers of margaritas and salt the glasses.

✔ **SMALL BUT IMPORTANT DETAIL.** Open the tonic and club sodas (then tightly reclose them) to prevent carbonation explosions at the bar.

✔ **POUR OURSELVES A SIGNATURE COCKTAIL.** We deserve it after all we've accomplished!

OPEN-MIKE NIGHT

Finish this song lyric: *But when I get home to you, I find the things that you do. . . .* You probably not only know the rest of the line (*. . . will make me feel all right*), you may now be singing "A Hard Day's Night" in your head, even if the Beatles broke up before you were born. Music, more than any other kind of pop culture knowledge, seems to stick with us. Everybody has a secret brain compartment filled with bits and pieces of song lyrics, from TV themes to Broadway tunes to Top 40 hits you're embarrassed you remember so well. At the Open-Mike party, it takes only a cocktail or two and a couple of backup singers—in the form of fellow guests—to tap into it.

CONVERSATION
KICK-STARTER

The gist: You prompt the songfest with a collection of paper coasters with song lyrics written on the front and the song title and performer on the back. Guests will try to guess the supplied answers, but they'll also find themselves trying to remember the next line, confessing that, yes, they went to every Air Supply concert, and of course, breaking into song.

The logistics: When we throw this party for our mostly 30-something crowd, we tend to go heavy on the '80s tunes, not only because they're what our friends know but also because they're an excellent source of hilariously horrible lyrics. But if your guests will have more fun with hip-hop, songs from the '60s, country music, or everything Elvis ever sang, no problem: The Internet's got them all. We Googled "Top 40 hits of the '80s," which reminded us of old favorites by artists like Bon Jovi and Prince. When we had a list of songs we knew would resonate with our guests, we searched on the song name or band name and "lyrics" and came up with multiple Web sites that gave us the complete words to every tune. It took us less than 20 seconds to come up with "I'm on the hunt I'm after you" for the front of one coaster, for example. Very few of our guests had to turn it over to see the name of the song: "Hungry Like The Wolf," a Duran Duran classic. (And if that song is now stuck in your head, all we can say is See? Song lyrics are infectious!)

We recommend having at least 25 different lyric-imprinted coasters (you'll find paper coasters at party-supply stores), sorted into stacks of five or so and placed around the room. We've never found it necessary to make more than that—guests always begin tossing out favorite song lines on their own, frequently while accompanying themselves on air guitar or air drums. (There are lots of invisible microphones at this party, too.)

THE INSPIRATION FOR THIS *fruity, juicy drink was the classic Singapore Sling. Our version has just the right amount of sweetness without distracting from the food.*

SING-SOME-MORE SLING

TO MAKE ONE DRINK:

$\frac{1}{2}$ **ounce gin**

$\frac{1}{2}$ **ounce cherry brandy**

$\frac{1}{2}$ **ounce Cointreau**

$\frac{1}{2}$ **ounce fresh lime juice**

$\frac{3}{4}$ **ounce orange juice**

$\frac{3}{4}$ **ounce pineapple juice**

club soda

maraschino cherry

SHAKE the first six ingredients with ice and strain into an ice-filled glass. Top off with a splash of club soda and a maraschino cherry.

TO MAKE A PITCHER (ABOUT 20 DRINKS):

$1\frac{1}{4}$ **cups gin**

$1\frac{1}{4}$ **cups cherry brandy**

$1\frac{1}{4}$ **cups Cointreau**

$1\frac{1}{4}$ **cups fresh lime juice**

2 cups orange juice

2 cups pineapple juice

$1\frac{1}{2}$ **liters club soda**

maraschino cherries

COMBINE all the ingredients except the club soda and cherries in a large pitcher, add ice, and stir for about 30 seconds. Spoon out the ice cubes. Store the pitcher in the refrigerator until party time. As you pour each drink, top it off with club soda and a maraschino cherry.

THE MENU

Reward your guests—they're singing for their supper!

Baby Lamb Chops with Rosemary Mustard Cream

Shrimp and Polenta Wedges

Sweet Potato Spread

Tomato-Basil-Mozzarella Skewers with Basil Oil

Champagne-Marinated Grapes

Recipes

baby lamb chops with rosemary mustard cream

MAKES SLIGHTLY LESS THAN 1 CUP OF ROSEMARY MUSTARD CREAM, ENOUGH FOR 15 TO 20 LAMB CHOPS

At Easter, our family traditionally serves leg of lamb, which we love, with mint jelly, which we . . . don't love. So we substituted this rich mustard sauce a year or so ago, and it was such a big hit at Easter dinner that we adapted the entire dish as an hors d'oeuvre.

FOR THE MUSTARD CREAM

½ cup dry white wine*

¼ cup chopped shallots

1 cup whipping cream

2 tablespoons Dijon mustard

2 teaspoons finely chopped rosemary

salt and pepper

FOR THE LAMB CHOPS

garlic cloves

baby lamb chops, enough to have 1½ chops per guest**

salt and pepper

olive oil for cooking

PREPARE THE MUSTARD CREAM: In a small saucepan, boil the white wine and shallots over high heat until liquid is reduced to about ¼ cup, about 5 minutes. Reduce heat to medium and add whipping cream. Simmer until sauce is slightly thickened, about 30 minutes (you should have slightly less than 1 cup sauce). Add the mustard and rosemary and simmer 2 minutes to blend flavors. Add salt and pepper to taste.

* *For this recipe and most others that call for dry white wine, an under-$10 bottle of Chardonnay or Pinot Grigio is fine. Or if you're serving white wine at your party, use that.*

** *Ask your butcher (or meat-case guy) to French the chops for you, meaning to remove the extra flesh along the bone so that you have a nice clean "handle." You can do this yourself by scraping along the bone with a paring knife, but it's tedious.*

PREHEAT broiler.

PREPARE THE LAMB CHOPS: Cut a garlic clove in half and rub the cut side on both sides of each lamb chop (every fourth or fifth chop, cut a new garlic clove). Sprinkle the chops liberally with salt and pepper. Lightly oil a large skillet and heat over medium-high heat. Sear the chops on both sides to brown them. Transfer them to a broiling pan and broil about 4 inches from the flame for about 3 minutes, then turn them over and broil another 3 minutes, for medium-rare.

SERVE THE LAMB CHOPS with the sauce alongside (and spreaders, so guests don't have to double-dip). Provide a bowl for discarded bones.

make-ahead factor: *The mustard cream sauce can be made up to 2 days ahead and kept covered and refrigerated. Bring to room temperature before serving.*

easy menus for entertaining outdoors

When the weather's nice, we're all for moving any party outside—there's something about being in the backyard or on the roof or at a tree-filled park that makes a party feel extra-festive and gives guests license to really kick back and relax. Your biggest challenge as the host: Creating an easy, serve-at-room-temperature menu that doesn't require proximity to the kitchen or the availability of electrical outlets. We've created three menus from recipes throughout the book that make outdoor entertaining a breeze:

MENU #1

Pork Tenderloin Sandwiches Two Ways (p. 92)

Peppery Shrimp (p. 108)

Smoked Trout Spread (p. 40)

Crostini with Tapenade (p. 83)

Any of the bowl foods in one large bowl

MENU #2

Tandoori Lamb with Cumin Dipping Sauce (p. 80)

Shrimp with Spicy Lime Dip (p. 157)

Cucumber Goat Cheese Spread (p. 111)

Fresh Tomato Bruschetta (p. 73)

Any of the bowl foods in one large bowl

MENU #3

Chicken and Red Onion in Phyllo Cups (p. 69)

Seared Tuna and Cucumber Brochettes (p. 94)

Creamy Crab Dip with Jicama Spears (p. 126)

Sun-dried Tomato and Ricotta Torte Trio (p. 95)

Any of the bowl foods in one large bowl

shrimp and polenta wedges

Both of us spent several years living in North Carolina, though at different times. Our mutual favorite meal while we were there was the shrimp and grits at Crook's Corner in Chapel Hill. Once we moved up north, we adapted it into a party-friendly finger food using polenta.

FOR THE SHRIMP

6 slices bacon, diced

olive oil for cooking

1 pound medium shrimp, peeled, deveined, and roughly chopped

1 large garlic clove, minced

3½ cups diced white mushrooms

1½ cups sliced scallions (white and pale green parts)

4 teaspoons fresh lemon juice

2 dashes Tabasco sauce, or more to taste

salt and pepper

FOR THE POLENTA

butter for greasing the pan

4 cups chicken stock

2 cups quick-cooking polenta

2 cups grated sharp Cheddar cheese

½ teaspoon salt

¼ teaspoon white pepper

pinch cayenne

pinch ground nutmeg

PREPARE THE SHRIMP: In a large skillet, cook the bacon over medium heat until brown around the edges but not too crisp, 5 to 6 minutes. Drain on paper towels and set aside. Add enough olive oil to the bacon fat in the skillet to make a thin layer. Add the chopped shrimp. Sauté until pink and just cooked through, 2 to 3 minutes. Remove from pan and set aside.

IF THE PAN IS DRY add another tablespoon of olive oil. Add garlic and sauté for about 1 minute. Add the mushrooms and sauté, stirring frequently, until softened, about 4 minutes. Add the scallions and sauté until wilted, another 1 to 2 minutes. Return the shrimp and bacon to the skillet, sprinkle with the lemon juice and Tabasco, and stir until combined. Add salt and pepper to taste. Set aside.

BUTTER a 13 x 9 x 2 inch pan.

PREPARE THE POLENTA: In a large saucepan, bring the chicken stock to a boil. Slowly add the polenta, stirring constantly. Continue to cook, stirring constantly, for another 1 to 1½ minutes, until thickened. Add the cheese, salt, pepper, cayenne, and nutmeg and stir until the cheese is incorporated, about 30 seconds.

IMMEDIATELY ADD the shrimp mixture. Stir until thoroughly mixed, then remove from heat. Spread the mixture in the buttered pan. Let it sit for 5 to 10 minutes to firm up. Cut into 1½-inch squares, then diagonally across the squares to form triangles. Serve warm.

make-ahead factor: *The shrimp can be made 1 day ahead and kept covered and refrigerated. The squares can be cut 1 day ahead and kept covered and refrigerated. Warm them in a 350°F oven for 12 to 15 minutes.*

SISTERS' SECRETS TO CONFIDENT HOSTESSING
what to expect from your guests every time

No matter what the occasion or who your guests, they're going to do the following three things at some point during the evening. Preparing for them from the get-go makes it much less frustrating when they happen:

1. GUESTS WILL CONGREGATE IN THE KITCHEN. Don't stress about whether the kitchen is spotless—it won't be, it can't be, and we suspect that its very informality is what draws people there in the first place. If you really need some elbow room, put plates of hors d'oeuvres in your guests' hands and send them out to feed the masses.

2. THEY WILL BREAK OR SPILL SOMETHING OR BOTH. We've never had a party where all the glasses survived—which is why we don't use fine crystal and we always have our Dustbuster charged up. The main thing is not to make the spiller or breaker feel bad. Dismiss apologies with a "Hey, it's not a party until someone breaks a glass!" Swiftly sweep up the mess and let the incident go. Hey, it's not a party until someone breaks a glass.

3. PEOPLE WILL SNEAK A PEEK INSIDE YOUR MEDICINE CABINET. C'mon, you know you've done it, too. If you've got a lip-waxing kit or Rogaine stash you don't want your guests to discover, you need a better hiding place than that middle shelf!

sweet potato spread

MAKES 3 CUPS OF SPREAD

This slightly sweet spread is a big draw at one of our favorite neighborhood restaurants, so we were thrilled when we found a version of the recipe in a local magazine. Our clipping doesn't say what the source is, but we can tell you the name of the restaurant—Josie's—and recommend you go there if you're in New York City.

3 large sweet potatoes (about 2 pounds), peeled and cut into 1-inch cubes

2 medium carrots, peeled and finely chopped

1 small yellow onion, finely chopped

2 tablespoons tahini*

¾ teaspoon salt

¼ teaspoon curry powder

¼ teaspoon ground cumin

focaccia bread

PREHEAT oven to 400°F.

PLACE THE SWEET POTATOES in a shallow roasting pan or jelly-roll pan and cover with foil. Roast potatoes for 15 minutes. Uncover and continue roasting until tender and soft, about another 30 minutes.

WHILE POTATOES ARE ROASTING, combine the carrots, onion, and ½ cup water in a medium nonstick skillet. Bring to a boil; reduce the heat and simmer covered for 5 minutes. Uncover and cook until water evaporates and vegetables are tender, about 3 minutes.

IN A FOOD PROCESSOR, combine the sweet potatoes, tahini, salt, curry powder, and cumin. Process until smooth. Gradually add enough remaining water to make a spreadable puree. Add carrot mixture and pulse until blended. Serve at room temperature or chilled, with wedges of focaccia.

make-ahead factor: *The dip can be made 4 days ahead and kept covered and refrigerated, or made up to 2 weeks ahead and frozen.*

* *Tahini is ground sesame seeds. In the supermarket, look for it near the soy sauce and sesame oil.*

tomato-basil-mozzarella skewers with basil oil

MAKES ABOUT 50 SKEWERS

This is the hors d'oeuvre version of the classic Italian Caprese salad. It's simple, it's elegant, and it adds a nice splash of color to a buffet table.

FOR THE BASIL OLIVE OIL

¼ cup (packed) fresh basil leaves

¼ cup olive oil

FOR THE SKEWERS

1 pint grape or cherry tomatoes (about 50), cut in half

50 small basil leaves

1½ pounds fresh buffalo mozzarella, cut into bite-size pieces

salt and pepper

PREPARE THE BASIL OLIVE OIL: Roughly chop the basil leaves and add to the olive oil. Let infuse for at least 2 hours or overnight.

ASSEMBLE THE SKEWERS: Slide a tomato half, a basil leaf, a piece of mozzarella, and then another tomato half onto each skewer. Place the skewers on a serving dish and drizzle the basil olive oil over the skewers. Sprinkle with salt and pepper. Serve the remaining olive oil in a small dish alongside.

LOW EFFORT: Purchase a basil-infused olive oil from a gourmet food store.

MO' EFFORT: Make a slightly fancier version of the basil oil by blanching the basil leaves; it takes a little more time, but it keeps the basil bright green, lending a lovely color to the olive oil. Use the same ingredients and proportions in the recipe above for this variation: Bring medium saucepan of water to boil. Add basil and blanch 20 seconds. Drain. Transfer leaves to processor and blend well. With machine running, add oil through feed tube and blend until smooth. Season with salt and pepper. Let stand 3 hours at room temperature.

make-ahead factor: *Both make-at-home versions of the basil olive oil can be made 3 days ahead and kept covered and refrigerated. Bring to room temperature before serving.*

champagne-marinated grapes

Guests are sometimes surprised to find bowls of grapes around the room, so we sprinkle them with superfine sugar and lemon zest to signal that they have a little something extra. This is our adaptation of a *Bon Appetit* recipe for grapes marinated in white wine—champagne seems to give the grapes' flavor a little sparkle.

2 pounds red seedless grapes

3 cups dry Champagne or sparkling wine

1/4 cup sugar

1 tablespoon grated lemon peel, plus more for garnish

2 tablespoons superfine sugar

CUT THE BUNCHES OF GRAPES into smaller clusters of 2 to 4 grapes each. Pour the Champagne into a large plastic bowl with a tight-fighting lid. Add the sugar and lemon peel and stir gently until sugar is dissolved. Add the grapes, cover, and chill 8 hours or overnight.

POUR OFF THE MARINADE (some of the lemon zest will cling to the grapes). Gently blot the grapes dry with a paper towel and sprinkle them with the superfine sugar and more lemon peel if desired. Mound them into bowls.

make-ahead factor: *The grapes can be left in the marinade overnight. Once removed from the marinade, they'll keep in the refrigerator in a resealable plastic bag for 1 week.*

CALLING ALL
BEACH BUMS
An island idyll

A cocktail party is like a miniature vacation from real life—especially if it has a get-away-from-it-all desert island theme. Prime everyone with a fruity drink, play a little steel-band music, and everybody will be in laid-back vacation mode in no time.

CONVERSATION
KICK-STARTER

The gist: To get guests talking, we give out blank stickers on the way in and ask everyone to jot down "3 Things I'd Want on a Desert Island" (Lauren's list: artichokes, Lyle Lovett CDs, the *New York Times* Sunday crossword puzzle. Anne's list: her husband RJ, a full season of *This Old House* on video, and Milano cookies).

The logistics: This one couldn't be simpler. You need pens and stickers (get the "Hello my name is" size, but without the words). Buy a generous supply of stickers. Guests have been known to change their minds mid-evening about what they can't live without: Our friend Amanda, a confirmed Manolos-and-manicures city girl, chose Kiehl's lip balm, a string bikini, and 300-thread-count sheets as her desert island necessities. Then she met our rugged-outdoors friend Jack, who was off to *his* desert island with a handheld GPS, a barrel of fresh water, and a flare gun. By 9 p.m., Amanda's sticker had a fourth item: Jack.

PICTURE YOURSELF *sitting at a tiki bar on a tropical island, sipping a delicious, fruity, frozen cocktail out of a hollowed-out coconut embellished with an umbrella. Now remove all of the trappings except the delicious fruity part, and you've got the signature drink for this party. No blender noise, no cracking open a coconut, no freeze headache.*

THE GILLIGAN

TO MAKE ONE DRINK:

> **1 ounce white rum**
>
> **$\frac{1}{2}$ ounce blackberry brandy**
>
> **1 ounce pineapple juice**
>
> **1 ounce fresh lime juice**
>
> **2 teaspoons simple syrup**
>
> **dash grenadine**

SHAKE all the ingredients with ice and strain into an ice-filled glass.

TO MAKE A PITCHER (ABOUT 20 DRINKS):

> **$2\frac{1}{2}$ cups white rum**
>
> **$2\frac{1}{2}$ cups pineapple juice**
>
> **$2\frac{1}{2}$ cups fresh lime juice**
>
> **$1\frac{1}{4}$ cups blackberry brandy**
>
> **$\frac{3}{4}$ cup plus 2 tablespoons simple syrup**
>
> **$2\frac{1}{2}$ teaspoons grenadine**

COMBINE all the ingredients in a large pitcher, add ice, and stir for about 30 seconds. Spoon out the ice cubes. Store the pitcher in the refrigerator until party time.

THE MENU

Island food (loosely interpreted)

Chicken Satay with Peanut Sauce

Coconut Curry Scallops

Pineapple Salsa with Plantain Chips

Chickpea Cilantro Dip

Macadamia Nuts

Recipes

chicken satay with peanut sauce

I n this recipe, marinating the chicken makes it super-tender, so it's easy to eat from a skewer. We've read instructions for soaking the wooden skewers in water to keep them from burning in the oven, but at the low cooking temperature in this recipe, ours have always been fine without soaking.

FOR THE CHICKEN

2 tablespoons dry white wine

1 tablespoon soy sauce

1 tablespoon cornstarch

3 large garlic cloves, minced

1 egg white

1/2 teaspoon dried red pepper flakes

1 pound boneless skinless chicken breasts, cut into strips 3 inches long, 1/2 inch wide

salt for sprinkling on the chicken

FOR THE PEANUT SAUCE

2 tablespoons toasted sesame oil

3 scallions, finely chopped (white and pale green parts)

2 garlic cloves, minced

1 tablespoon grated fresh ginger

1 cup water

1/2 cup high-quality creamy peanut butter

1/4 cup soy sauce

1/4 cup rice wine vinegar

2 tablespoons firmly packed brown sugar

1/4 teaspoon dried red pepper flakes

36 wooden skewers

PREPARE THE CHICKEN: Whisk the first six ingredients together in a medium bowl. Add the chicken and toss to coat. Cover and refrigerate for at least 2 hours.

PREHEAT oven to 350°F.

THREAD ONE STRIP OF CHICKEN onto each skewer accordion-style and place on a lightly oiled baking sheet. Bake until chicken is just cooked through, 10 to 12 minutes. Sprinkle lightly with salt.

PREPARE THE PEANUT SAUCE: In a saucepan, heat the sesame oil over moderate heat until hot. Add scallions, garlic, and ginger. Cook, stirring, until scallions are wilted, about 1 minute. Stir in water, peanut butter, soy sauce, vinegar, brown sugar, and red pepper flakes and bring to a simmer, stirring until the sauce is smooth. Remove from heat and cool to room temperature (it continues to thicken as it cools).

SERVE THE SKEWERS warm or at room temperature, with peanut sauce and a bowl or plate for discarded skewers.

NO EFFORT: Buy a commercial peanut sauce.

LOW EFFORT: Buy a commercial peanut sauce and soup it up a bit by whirring it in a food processor with ½ teaspoon soy sauce, ¼ cup creamy peanut butter, and 2 minced garlic cloves (adjust these amounts to taste).

make-ahead factor: *The chicken skewers can be assembled and cooked 1 day ahead and kept covered and refrigerated. Bring them to room temperature before serving. The peanut sauce can be made 3 days ahead and kept covered and refrigerated.*

SISTERS' SECRETS TO CONFIDENT HOSTESSING
How to up the fun without going over the top

There are those who believe that Costume Parties = Madcap Fun. We're in the other camp. On the other hand, a little *hint* of a costume can add a mood of exclusivity and camaraderie to a party, like knowing the secret handshake. The trick is to make the almost-costume something sexy and fun to wear, not something silly. For this island party, we would never make guests wear tacky (and scratchy!) plastic leis, for instance, but we do like to announce on the invitations that the party will be a flip-flops-only zone. For the map party on page 19, we've suggested that guests come in a souvenir t-shirt from a favorite vacation spot. Anything that makes the party unusual is great; anything that makes the guests uncomfortable is not.

coconut curry scallops

MAKES ABOUT 60 SCALLOPS

Coconut and curry put an unusual tropical spin on sweet, mild scallops. Guests can eat the scallops as served, with the rich, slightly spicy sauce drizzled over them, or they can add extra crunch by rolling the scallops in the toasted coconut.

1½ cups sweetened, flaked coconut

FOR THE COCONUT CURRY SAUCE

1 cup canned unsweetened coconut milk

2 tablespoons fresh lime juice

1 teaspoon curry powder

½ teaspoon salt

FOR THE SCALLOPS

1 pound sea scallops

¾ cup flour

1 tablespoon grated lime zest

½ teaspoon salt

¼ teaspoon freshly ground black pepper

2 tablespoons peanut oil

PREHEAT oven to 350°F.

TOAST THE COCONUT: Spread the coconut on a baking sheet. Toast 8 to 10 minutes, stirring every 2 to 3 minutes, until lightly browned (watch it carefully toward the end of the baking time). Set aside.

PREPARE THE SAUCE: Mix all the ingredients in a saucepan. Simmer over low to medium heat until thickened, about 15 minutes. Remove from the heat and set aside.

PREPARE THE SCALLOPS: Remove the small muscle from the side of each scallop if it feels tough to the touch. Slice each scallop in half horizontally. Pat the scallops dry with a paper towel. Combine the flour, lime zest, salt, and pepper in a shallow bowl. Dredge each scallop in the flour mixture and tap gently to remove excess flour.

IN A SAUTÉ PAN, heat the oil over medium-high heat until very hot. Working in batches, sauté the scallops until cooked through on the inside and deep brown on the outside, about 1 minute per side. Keep the cooked scallops warm on a baking tray in a 200°F oven.

ON A SERVING PLATTER, arrange the scallops and drizzle the coconut-curry sauce over them. Place the remaining sauce on the side for dipping. Put the toasted coconut on a shallow plate next to the platter. Provide toothpicks.

make-ahead factor: *The coconut can be toasted 4 to 5 days ahead and kept tightly covered at room temperature. The coconut-curry sauce can be made 3 days ahead and kept covered and refrigerated. It partially solidifies when cold, so let it return to room temperature and stir well to recombine before drizzling it over the scallops.*

SISTERS' SECRETS TO CONFIDENT HOSTESSING
How to gracefully end a party

We've been to parties where, at 1 or 2 a.m., the weary, bleary hostess has turned on all the lights, killed the music, and bellowed, "Everybody out!" Effective, but not endearing. You want your guests to leave wishing the party could go on all night, not feeling as though they've been bounced out into the street mid-martini. Use our gradual get-'em-out strategy to gently wind down the evening while keeping the party glow going.

About 30 minutes before you want the party to end, issue the gracious-hostess version of last call. Make the rounds, asking if you can get anybody "one last drink," then put the liquor away, empty the ice buckets, and shut down the bar. Pause and have one last drink yourself, if you like.

About 15 minutes later, begin collecting empty plates and glasses from around the room and making general clean-up motions. Potential benefit: Someone might actually help you—and the more people who help you, the bigger the hint to the rest of the guests that it's time to head home.

zero hour. If you've still got hangers-on who seem content to make your sofa their final resting place, blow out the candles and turn off the music (keep it gentle: dial down the volume, then turn it off). This almost never fails to clear the room, but there's a step 4 just in case . . . .

last resort: Guests who haven't said *ciao* by now are clearly beyond hint-taking capacity. Thank them warmly for "staying until the end," helpfully hand them their coats or purses or umbrellas, and hold the front door open until they've walked through it.

pineapple salsa with plantain chips

MAKES ABOUT $2\frac{1}{2}$ CUPS OF SALSA

Stranded in the Tampa International Airport one weekend, we picked up a cook-book called *The Special Taste of Florida* (as well as some grapefruit wine, but that was our less successful purchase). The book attributes this salsa recipe to the Beech Street Grill in Fernandina Beach, Florida. Broiling the pineapple deepens its flavor and keeps the salsa from being too sweet.

1 pineapple, peeled, cored, and sliced into $\frac{1}{4}$-inch-thick rounds

1 tablespoon olive oil

cup chopped red onion

$\frac{1}{2}$ cup chopped red bell pepper

2 tablespoons brown sugar

$\frac{1}{4}$ cup chopped scallions (white and pale green parts)

2 tablespoons chopped cilantro, or more to taste

2 tablespoons fresh lime juice

2 tablespoons red wine vinegar

purchased plantain chips

PREHEAT broiler.

BROIL THE PINEAPPLE SLICES in the oven, about 4 minutes per side, until brown along edges. Remove from heat and let cool slightly, then finely dice.

HEAT THE OLIVE OIL over medium heat, add the onion, and stir for 3 to 4 minutes, until onion is softened but not browned. Add the red pepper and the brown sugar and stir for 1 minute to combine. Remove from heat and add to pineapple. Add the scallions, cilantro, lime juice, and vinegar. Stir to combine. Refrigerate until an hour before party time. Serve with plantain chips.

make-ahead factor: *The salsa can be prepared up to 4 days ahead and kept covered and refrigerated. Remove it from the fridge an hour before serving—the flavors are better at room temperature.*

chickpea cilantro dip

This is a nice variation on hummus. The cilantro adds a fresh, grassy-in-a-good-way flavor to the chickpeas and yogurt lightens the whole thing up.

2 cups canned chickpeas, rinsed and drained

²/₃ cup loosely packed fresh cilantro leaves

¹/₂ cup plain yogurt

3 tablespoons fresh lemon juice

1 large garlic clove, chopped

¹/₂ teaspoon salt

¹/₄ teaspoon pepper

IN A FOOD PROCESSOR, puree the ingredients until smooth. Let the dip sit for at least an hour to let the flavors meld.

SERVE WITH CRACKERS, toasted pita wedges, crudités, or all three.

make-ahead factor: *The dip can be made 2 days ahead and kept covered and refrigerated. Remove it from the fridge at least an hour before party time—it tastes best at or near room temperature.*

macadamia nuts

Mound whole, salted macadamia nuts in bowls around the party space. Piece of cake!

A MOVEABLE FEAST
A 3-country, 3-cocktail party

In this creative take on the progressive party, guests travel among three countries just by hopping from house to house. At each place, the signature cocktail, hors d'oeuvres, and music reflect a chosen locale, which keeps guests involved and curious to see what comes next. In a quirky homage to Ernest Hemingway, for instance, we created a party based on places he lived—Key West, Paris, and Havana—but you and your fellow hosts can choose any three places you'd like to spend an evening.

Conversation
KICK-STARTER

The gist: Physically moving the party from place to place works on the guests much the way shaking works on a cocktail—it mixes and remixes them. As the party-goers arrive at each spot, the ever-changing ambience creates fresh topics of conversation and new opportunities to mingle. In addition, sharing the role of host does more than just ease the pre-party workload; it makes for an interesting mix of party-goers, since the guest list is a joint production.

The logistics: First, of course, you need to get three hosts to agree on a date for the party, but that's really the only hard part. Next, decide which city each host will be responsible for. We structure our evening so that guests spend about an hour and a half at the first home (Key West), which gives stragglers time to arrive. The food is fairly light. At the second home (Paris), they spend about an hour. The food is a little heavier here. Then onto the final stop (Havana), where there are substantial sandwiches and arepas, and the guests can settle in for the rest of the evening. In order to keep the partygoers together as they travel from home to home, print out the three addresses (and walking or driving directions, if necessary) and put a stack at each party. It's also nice to include the menu, so that guests will see at a glance that, say, there will be hors d'oeuvres heavy enough to make dinner out of, or that they can walk from Home #2 to Home #3 (which means they can have another daiquiri).

Since each host has only two hors d'oeuvres and a signature cocktail to prepare, he or she can devote more energy to playing up the theme of the party. Music is one easy way to do that. There were some obvious choices for our party: Jimmy Buffett in Key West, Edith Piaf in Paris, and the Buena Vista Social Club soundtrack in Havana. We also had fun with the décor, displaying Hemingway books and even borrowing a mounted moose head in a nod to his big-game-hunter days.

KEY WEST: FLORIDA PUNCH

DURING HIS YEARS *in Key West, Hemingway drank at Sloppy Joe's Bar. Though there's no evidence he ever ordered this citrusy punch, we feel sure it would have met with his approval: It packs a Hemingway-worthy wallop.*

TO MAKE ONE DRINK:

- 1 ounce white rum
- 1 ounce brandy
- 1 ounce Rose's Lime Juice
- 2 ounces grapefruit juice

SHAKE all the ingredients with ice and strain into an ice-filled glass.

TO MAKE A PITCHER (ABOUT 20 DRINKS):

- $2^{1}/_{2}$ cups white rum
- $2^{1}/_{2}$ cups brandy
- $2^{1}/_{2}$ cups Rose's Lime Juice
- 5 cups grapefruit juice

COMBINE all the ingredients in a large pitcher, add ice, and stir for about 30 seconds. Spoon out the ice cubes. Store the pitcher in the refrigerator until party time.

PARIS: THE LEFT BANK

THIS WINE-BASED COCKTAIL *is named for the bank of the Seine where Hemingway's Parisian hangout, Café Les Deux Magots, is located.*

TO MAKE ONE DRINK:

- 1 ounce orange-flavored vodka
- $^{3}/_{4}$ ounce red wine
- $^{1}/_{2}$ ounce triple sec
- $^{1}/_{2}$ ounce orange juice
- $^{1}/_{4}$ ounce lime juice

SHAKE all the ingredients with ice and strain into a martini glass. The drink can also be served on the rocks.

TO MAKE A PITCHER (ABOUT 20 DRINKS):

- $2^{1}/_{2}$ cups orange-flavored vodka
- $1^{3}/_{4}$ cups plus 2 tablespoons red wine
- $1^{1}/_{4}$ cups triple sec
- $1^{1}/_{4}$ cups orange juice
- $^{1}/_{2}$ cup plus 2 tablespoons lime juice

COMBINE all the ingredients in a large pitcher, add ice, and stir for about 30 seconds. Spoon out the ice cubes. Store the pitcher in the refrigerator until party time.

HAVANA: DAIQUIRI

AT HIS FAVORITE HAVANA BAR, *La Floridita, Hemingway became known as Papa Dobles because he always ordered double daiquiris. His preferred daiquiri included grapefruit juice and maraschino liqueur (if you're a stickler for authenticity, the recipe is easily found on the Internet). We love this simpler version, which is a better foil for the food.*

TO MAKE ONE DRINK:

- $1^{1}/_{2}$ ounces white rum
- 1 ounce fresh lime juice
- $1^{1}/_{2}$ teaspoons simple syrup

SHAKE all the ingredients with ice and strain into an ice-filled glass.

TO MAKE A PITCHER (ABOUT 20 DRINKS):

- $3^{3}/_{4}$ cups white rum
- $2^{1}/_{2}$ cups fresh lime juice
- $^{1}/_{2}$ cup plus 2 tablespoons simple syrup

COMBINE all the ingredients in a large pitcher, add ice, and stir for about 30 seconds. Spoon out the ice cubes. Store the pitcher in the refrigerator until party time.

THE MENU

Since food is served in three homes, two hors d'oeuvres at each stop are plenty.

key west

Shrimp with Spicy Lime Dip

Hearts of Palm

paris

Tomato Sage Baby Brioches

Caramelized Onion Tarts

havana

Arepas with Pink Pickled Onions

Cuban Sandwiches Pequeños

in bowls at every party

Potato Chips

Recipes

shrimp with spicy lime dip

MAKES 40 TO 50 SHRIMP AND 1½ CUPS OF DIP

Making a dish ahead is often as good for the dish as it is for the cook. This dip needs at least an hour in the refrigerator in order for the flavors to meld, and overnight is even better, so be sure to allow time. If you're having an outdoor party, or you just don't care about mess, you can let the guests peel the shrimp themselves, saving you prep time.

FOR THE SHRIMP

1 pound medium shrimp

2 garlic cloves, crushed

FOR THE DIP

1 cup mayonnaise

½ cup sour cream

3 scallions, thinly sliced (white and pale green parts)

2 medium garlic cloves, minced

3 small chipotle chiles in adobo, minced to a paste, plus ½ teaspoon adobo sauce*

1 teaspoon grated lime zest plus 1 table-spoon juice (1 lime)

PREPARE THE SHRIMP: Peel the shrimp and devein them, if desired. Put the garlic clove in a pot of generously salted water and bring water to a boil. Put shrimp in and cook until they're pink and cooked through, about 3 minutes. (The water may not return to a boil in that time.) Chill in the refrigerator until ready to serve.

MAKE THE DIP: Mix all the ingredients in a small bowl until smooth and creamy. Refrigerate at least 1 hour.

make-ahead factor: *The dip can be made 3 days ahead and kept covered and refrigerated. The spice level tends to intensify over time, so you may want to start out with fewer chipotle chiles if you're going to prepare the dip ahead. The boiled and peeled shrimp can be kept covered and refrigerated for 1 day.*

* *The chiles are sold in cans. In the supermarket, look for them near the salsas.*

hearts of palm

MAKES ABOUT 50 PIECES

Hearts of palm—literally, the centers of young palm trees—have a smooth texture and a delicate flavor, somewhat like artichoke hearts. We've served them with both of the dips we suggest below, and you may find guests using the spicy lime dip (from the shrimp recipe on page 157) as well.

> 1 (14-ounce) can hearts of palm
> Lemon Dipping Sauce (page 41)
> Red Curry Mayonnaise (page 92)

DRAIN THE HEARTS OF PALM, rinse them with cold water, and blot dry with paper towels. Cut into ¼-inch slices.

PREPARE the dipping sauce of your choice.

SET OUT THE SLICES of hearts of palm alongside the dip. Provide toothpicks for spearing.

make-ahead factor: *Each of the dips can be made ahead of time. Check the specific recipe. The hearts of palm can be sliced 2 days ahead and kept covered and refrigerated.*

tomato sage baby brioches

MAKES ABOUT 36 BRIOCHES

This is comfort food with class: Eggs, cheese, and bread create a savory base. Fresh tomatoes and sage bring it up to cocktail-party standards.

2 tablespoons plus 1 teaspoon all-purpose flour	butter for buttering the baking dish
¾ teaspoon baking powder	1 loaf brioche or other dense white bread, cut into ½-inch-thick slices with crusts removed
1½ teaspoons kosher salt	
3 large eggs	1½ cups diced tomato
1 ⅓ cups milk	½ cup diced onion
1½ cups grated extra sharp white cheddar cheese	⅓ cup finely chopped fresh sage
	½ teaspoon minced garlic

PREHEAT oven to 350°F.

IN A SMALL BOWL, combine flour, baking powder, and salt and set aside. In a large bowl, whisk together the eggs and the milk. Add the flour mixture and whisk until the batter is smooth. Stir in the cheese.

GENEROUSLY BUTTER a 13 x 9 x 2 baking dish. Dip the bread slices into the egg and cheese mixture, coating both sides. Arrange the slices side by side in the pan, keeping the bread in a single layer. Cut the bread to fit if needed. Set aside.

STIR the tomatoes, onion, sage, and garlic into the remaining egg batter. Spread evenly over the bread slices.

BAKE until golden brown, 30 to 40 minutes. Let cool for 5 to 10 minutes before cutting with a 1½-inch cookie cutter into rounds. Serve warm.

LOW EFFORT: Cut the brioches into squares instead of using the cookie cutter. Only slightly less cute and just as delicious.

make-ahead factor: *The brioches can be made up to 2 days ahead and kept refrigerated. Reheat on a baking sheet in a 250°F oven for 10 minutes, placing them close together to keep them moist.*

caramelized onion tarts

MAKES ABOUT 96 TARTS

This is our interpretation of the classic French pissaladière. Ours is both easier to make and easier to pronounce.

FOR THE TART CRUSTS

1 package frozen puff pastry (2 sheets), thawed according to package directions

1 egg, beaten to make egg wash

olive oil for oiling the baking sheet

FOR THE TOPPING

2 tablespoons olive oil

4 medium yellow onions, thinly sliced

1/2 teaspoon kosher salt

1 cup crumbled feta cheese

PREPARE THE TART CRUSTS: Unfold the pastry sheets and cut each one along the fold lines, creating three tarts from each sheet, each about 3 inches wide. (Work with one sheet at a time, keeping the second sheet chilled, covered with plastic wrap.) Fold up about 1/2 inch of the edge of each tart to create a "crust." Brush the entire tart with egg wash and prick the dough all over with the tines of a fork. Cover and refrigerate the uncooked tarts for 20 minutes until firm.

PREHEAT oven to 400°F.

BAKE THE TARTS on a lightly oiled baking sheet for 12 to 15 minutes or until golden brown and flaky throughout (be sure the tart crust isn't still doughy in the middle). Repeat with remaining pastry sheet.

PREPARE THE TOPPING: Heat the olive oil in a large saucepan over medium heat. Add the onions and salt. Cook, stirring occasionally, until the onions are golden in color and soft, 30 to 40 minutes.

ASSEMBLE THE TARTS: Spread equal amounts of the caramelized onions and feta cheese over each baked tart, pricking the centers of the tart crusts with a fork if necessary to "depuff" them. Place assembled tarts back in the oven for 10 to 12 minutes to warm the toppings through.

SLICE EACH TART crosswise into pieces about 1 inch wide.

LOW EFFORT: Instead of the caramelized onions, substitute other traditional pissaladière ingredients that don't require cooking: 1 cup chopped black olives and 1 cup diced tomatoes. That cuts out 40 minutes of cooking time.

MO' EFFORT: Make an assortment of tarts with various toppings. In addition to the caramelized onion-feta cheese combo, and the black olive-tomato variation, we love the following combinations of ingredients (you'll need about ½ cup of cheese and 1 cup of vegetables for each tart):

> Gruyère cheese with diced artichoke hearts
> Brie with sun-dried tomatoes
> Goat cheese with roasted red peppers

make-ahead factor: *The tarts without toppings can be made up to 2 days ahead and kept tightly covered at room temperature. The onions can be cooked 3 to 4 days ahead and kept covered and refrigerated. Assemble the tarts no more than 3 hours before the party and warm them on a baking sheet in a 400°F oven for 8 to 10 minutes.*

arepas with pink pickled onions

We've taken these traditional corn pancakes and given them a more complex flavor with the addition of sour cream and a piquant pickled onion relish. The onions' wonderful rose-pink color against the golden-brown arepas makes for a gorgeous presentation.

FOR THE PICKLED ONIONS

2 medium red onions, finely chopped

½ cup cider vinegar

4 teaspoons sugar

½ teaspoon salt

FOR THE AREPAS

1 cup milk

5 tablespoons butter

1 cup frozen corn kernels

1 cup white arepa flour*

1 cup shredded mozzarella

1 tablespoon sugar

¼ teaspoon salt

½ cup water

2 tablespoons canola oil

sour cream for topping

PREPARE THE PICKLED ONIONS: Put the onions in a small saucepan with the vinegar, sugar, salt, and enough cold water to just cover them. Bring to a boil and simmer 5 minutes, stirring until the liquid evaporates (add a little more water if the liquid evaporates before the 5 minutes are up). Remove pan from heat.

PREPARE THE AREPAS: In a small saucepan, bring the milk to a boil. Add the butter and stir until it is melted. Remove the mixture from the heat and set aside.

IN A FOOD PROCESSOR, roughly grind the frozen corn kernels. In a large bowl, combine the corn, flour, mozzarella, sugar, and salt. Make a well in the middle of the flour mixture and gradually add the hot milk mixture, stirring to combine thoroughly. Gradually add ½ cup water, one tablespoon at a time, until the mixture has the consistency of thick pancake batter. (Use more water if necessary.)

---

* *This is also called white cornmeal. One widely available brand is Goya.*

HEAT THE CANOLA OIL in a skillet over low heat. Working in batches, spoon the arepas individually into the skillet, using a scant tablespoon of batter for each arepa. Each pancake should be about 2 inches across. Cook until golden brown and cooked through, about 5 minutes on each side. As you work, the batter will continue to thicken. Continue to add water a tablespoon at a time to the arepa mixture as needed to maintain pancake batter consistency.

TOP EACH AREPA with a swipe of sour cream and a dollop of pink pickled onions and arrange them on a tray or, if you're short on time, put out the sour cream and onions in separate bowls and let guests top the arepas themselves.

LOW EFFORT: If you don't have time to make the onions, simply serve the arepas with sour cream and prepared pickle relish.

make-ahead factor: *The pickled onions can be made 1 week ahead and kept covered and refrigerated. The arepa dough can be made 1 day ahead and kept covered and refrigerated. You'll need to add a little water to get it back to pancake batter consistency. The arepas can be made the morning of the party and kept tightly covered but not refrigerated. Warm them in a 400°F oven for 5 to 7 minutes.*

How to pull together a party on short notice

We'd all love party-throwing to be so effortless that you could feel free to entertain whenever the mood struck, but every successful party requires planning. To entertain frequently with minimum effort, repeat a party you've thrown before instead of starting from scratch each time.

The supposed Holy Grail of Hostesshood—being endlessly innovative and wowing your guests at every turn—is highly overrated. Of course, we encourage you to experiment, to add bells and whistles to your parties, to try out new dishes and drinks—for a host, part of the satisfaction of entertaining is exercising your creativity. But when it comes to your guests, never underestimate the allure of the familiar.

We throw the Wine-Tasting Party Even Beer Drinkers Will Love every December to celebrate Lauren's birthday. Guests who have been coming since the first one five years ago look forward to it every year and get a kick out of guiding first-timers through the tasting. And our jobs as hosts are made much easier since we can practically throw the party with our eyes closed.

Don't be afraid to recycle the food and drink recipes, too. There are entertaining gurus who would have you believe that serving an hors d'oeuvre to the same people twice is anathema. Baloney! If you've got a recipe you absolutely love that gets rave reviews, make it your signature. Several years ago, we made a note to ourselves that we'd served our Moroccan lamb meatballs several times and should substitute something new for the next party. Then that next party rolled around and guests complained! "What? No lamb meatballs? But I *love* your lamb meatballs!" We've since brought them out of retirement (page 24). Our mother gets the same reaction with her trademark margaritas—when she thinks everybody *must* be tired of them and she swaps in some fancy concoction, her guests protest (the recipe's on p. 118).

Having a few signature elements means at least part of your party-planning can be done practically on autopilot—and ironically, also cements your reputation as a hostess. So when a party is a success, throw it again. And again. And again. And by the way, we'd love to be invited.

cuban sandwiches pequeños

MAKES ABOUT 35 MINI SANDWICHES

In our hometown of Bartow, Florida, *the* place to get Cuban sandwiches was called Pedro's. In New York City, we've discovered a tiny Cuban takeout restaurant that makes them just like Pedro did—and for days when the restaurant is closed, we've learned how to make them ourselves. Here's our cocktail-party version.

2 loaves Cuban, French, or Italian bread*

prepared yellow mustard

12 thin dill pickle slices (dill "sandwich stackers" work perfectly)

$^{1}/_{2}$ pound roast pork, thinly sliced

$^{1}/_{2}$ pound baked ham, thinly sliced

$^{1}/_{4}$ pound salami, thinly sliced

$^{1}/_{2}$ pound Swiss cheese, thinly sliced

PREHEAT oven to 350°F.

SLICE THE BREAD HORIZONTALLY. Spread both sides with mustard. Layer the remaining ingredients in this order: pickles, roast pork, ham, salami, and cheese. Cut each sandwich in half and place the halves in a large skillet. Place a heavy skillet on top and press down to flatten (or use a sandwich press if you have one). You want to smash the sandwich, compressing the bread to about a third of its original size. Grill the sandwiches for 2 to 3 minutes on each side, until the cheese is just starting to melt and the bread is golden.

REMOVE FROM THE HEAT and cut the sandwiches into 1-inch-wide slices using a serrated knife. Place the slices on a baking sheet and place in the oven to heat through, about 10 minutes.

make-ahead factor: *The sandwiches can be grilled 1 day ahead and kept tightly wrapped and refrigerated. Warm them in a 350°F oven for 12 to 15 minutes.*

---

* *Basically, you're looking for the kind of soft bread you'd get a Subway sandwich on—not hard and crusty, like a baguette.*

potato chips

Serve any kind of potato chips you like, though we usually choose thick-cut because that makes for fewer crumbly bits in the bowls. When guests wonder what the Hemingway connection is, you can remind them: Papa spent his last years in Idaho.

INDEX